D0852006

THE BRAIN EXPLORER

PUZZLES, RIDDLES, ILLUSIONS, AND OTHER MENTAL ADVENTURES

PAT MURPHY, ELLEN KLAGES, LINDA SHORE, PEARL TESLER, AND THE

expl**O**ratorium

THE BRAIN EXPLORER

PUZZLES, RIDDLES, ILLUSIONS, AND OTHER MENTAL ADVENTURES

Illustrations by Jason Gorski

An Owl Book

Henry Holt and Company

New York

Henry Holt and Company, LLC.
Publishers since 1866
115 West 18th Street
New York, New York 10011

Henry Holt® is a registered trademark
of Henry Holt and Company, LLC.

Copyright © 1999 by The Exploratorium
Design and production © 1999 by Tolleson Design

All rights reserved.

Published in Canada by Fitzhenry & Whiteside Ltd.,
195 Allstate Parkway, Markham, Ontario L3R 4T8.

Library of Congress Cataloging-in-Publication Data
The brain explorer: puzzles, riddles, illusions, and other mental
    adventures / by Pat Murphy . . . [et al.].— 1st ed.
        p. cm.—(An Exploratorium science-at-home book)
    "An owl book."
    Includes index.
    Summary: A collection of puzzles and activities dealing with
       memory, math, verbal skills, and visual perception.
    ISBN 0-8050-4538-4 (pbk.: alk. paper)
    1. Puzzles—Juvenile literature. 2. Riddles—Juvenile literature. 3. Magic
      tricks—Juvenile literature. [1. Puzzles.] I. Murphy, Pat, 1955–   . II. Series.
  GV1493.B673 1991
  793.73—dc21   98-54605
                                    CIP
                                    AC

Henry Holt Books are available for special promotions and premiums. For details,
    contact: Director, Special Markets.

First Edition 1999

Production editing by Ellyn Hament
Design and production by Tolleson Design
Illustrations by Jason Gorski

All illustrations are by Jason Gorski, unless otherwise noted. Page 31 (top right, bottom left, bottom right)
and page 33 are from the Droodles home page, http://www.webonly.com/droodles © 1996, 1997, 1998 Leo
Valdes. Page 31 (top left) and page 32 are from *Droodles* by Roger Price, Price/Stern/Sloan, Inc., Los Angeles,
CA, © 1996 Roger Price. Page 47: top left, center right, and bottom right photos by Bill Bowers. Top center,
top right, center left, bottom left by Esther Kutnick. Pages 69 (bottom) and 70 (bottom): *Perception,* Scientific
American Books, © 1984 Irvin Rock. Page 70 (top) and page 74 (left): *Mindsights* by Roger N. Shepard © 1990,
reprinted with permission of W.H. Freeman and Company. Page 74 (right): From *Can You Believe Your Eyes* by
Richard Block and Harold Yukor, Brunner/Mazel, Inc., New York, NY © 1989.

Exploratorium® is a registered trademark and service mark of The Exploratorium.

Band-Aid® is a registered trademark of JOHNSON & JOHNSON.
Boggle® is a registered trademark of Hasbro, Inc.
Oreo® is a registered trademark of Nabisco.
Popsicle® is a registered trademark of Good Humor-Breyers Ice Cream.
Post-it™ is a trademark of 3M.
Scrabble® is a registered trademark. All intellectual property rights in and to the game are owned in
    the U.S.A. by Hasbro, Inc., and in Canada by Hasbro Canada Inc.
Snickers© is copyright Mars, Incorporated.
Walt Disney World® is a registered trademark of Disney.
Wheel of Fortune is produced by Columbia TriStar Television, a Sony Pictures Entertainment Company.
Xerox® is a registered trademark of Xerox Corporation.

Printed in the United States of America

10 9 8 7 6 5 4 3 2 1

In San Francisco, California, there's a building filled with flashing lights and machines that buzz and whir and exhibits you can mess with. It's the Exploratorium, a world-famous museum of science, art, and human perception.

WELCOME TO THE EXPLORATORIUM

Your class is on a field trip to the Exploratorium when you see a door that looks kind of interesting. You decide to explore . . .

CAUTION CAUTION

To Whom it May Concern:

The Exploratorium's Science-at-Home team is heading off on a dangerous expedition into unknown territory—the world inside your brain. If all goes well, we'll be traveling through the dark tunnels of Caverns of Memory and following the twisted paths of the Forest of Hidden Surprises to reach the mysterious Puzzle House.

Follow us if you dare. We'll be exploring some strange and interesting places and finding out about the weird stuff that goes on inside your head.

Look for our notebooks along the way. In them, you'll find experiments to try, puzzles to solve, illusions to fool your eyes, and tips that will help you at every step of the way.

In the Caverns of Memory, you'll pick up tricks that will help you remember what other people forget. That's handy whether you're trying to ace a spelling test, impress a friend with your knowledge of baseball statistics, or just remember to bring your lunch to school.

In the Forest of Many Returns, you'll find tips on how to win at Hangman, Tic-Tac-Toe, and other games. You'll find some great puzzles and discover the secrets behind optical illusions.

And when you reach the Puzzle House, you'll find lots more puzzles—and learn ways that you can solve them faster than any of your friends. You'll also discover how to make puzzles of your own!

Have fun! Good luck!

Signed,
The Science-at-Home Team

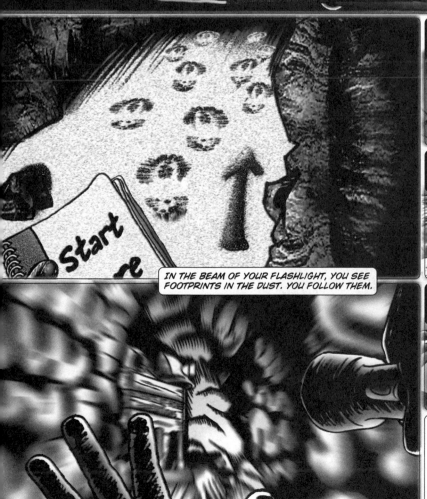

IN THE BEAM OF YOUR FLASHLIGHT, YOU SEE FOOTPRINTS IN THE DUST. YOU FOLLOW THEM.

To explore the Caverns of Memory, turn to page 8.

To explore the Forest of Hidden Surprises, turn to page 40.

To explore the Puzzle House, turn to page 90.

Solutions	132
Appendix 1: How to be a Good Puzzle and Problem Solver	128
Appendix 2: About Your Brain	130
Suggested Reading	139
Thank You Very Much!	140
Index	142
About the Exploratorium	144

CAVERNS OF MEMORY

The footsteps lead into a dark tunnel. You follow them through a maze of inter-connected caves. To explore any of these places, turn to the page number shown.

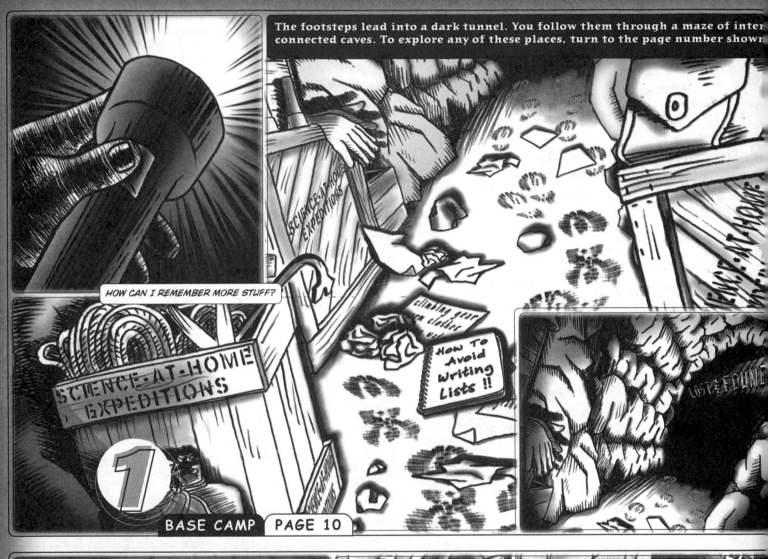

There's a dead flashlight beside a box of batteries locked with a combination lock. Looks like someone forgot the combination.

IS THERE A TRICK TO REMEMBERING NUMBERS?

3

COMBINATION CAVE PAGE 26

Add a riddle to a doodle and get a droodle!

WHY ARE SOME THINGS EASIER TO REMEMBER THAN OTHERS?

DROODLES
DROODLES

4

CAVE PAINTINGS PAGE 30

ALL THAT GLITTERS ISN'T GOLD!

You leave the treasure behind and stumble out into the moonlit night. To explore the Forest of Hidden Surprises, go to page 40.

WHY DOES MY MEMORY PLAY TRICKS?

5

TREASURE CHEST PAGE 34

9

HOW TO AVOID WRITING LISTS

There are kids out there who can name every president and vice president, in order. There are kids who know every dinosaur, its size and weight, and scientific name. There are kids who know all the players on their favorite baseball team and all their batting averages.

Some kids are like that. But even a kid who knows the winning team in every World Series since 1905 may have a hard time remembering a list of stuff to buy at the grocery store or the six words on this week's vocabulary list.

If your memory isn't as good as you'd like it to be, don't just say you have a rotten memory and give up. Here are some games that will help you remember lists of things, and some tricks that will help you amaze your friends with your astounding memory.

MEMORY PARTY GAME

Here's a game that tests your memory. Use this version if you want to play with a group of people. Play "Memory Solitaire" if you'd rather play alone.

20 things
2 minutes

WHAT DO I **NEED?**
• One person to be Game Master
• A few friends
• 20 different unrelated objects—like a pair of scissors, a can of beans, a hair brush, a pencil, and so on.
• A big towel that can cover the objects
• A clock or watch with a second hand
• A piece of paper and a pencil for each player

PARTY GAME

WHAT DO I **DO?**
1. Have the Game Master gather 20 different objects. If you're having a party, you can ask each person who's coming to bring something for the game. If you're playing with your family, each person could gather a few objects. These should be things that are not related to each other. You could have some things from the kitchen—like a can opener and a potato masher—and some from the bedroom—like a left shoe and a bow tie.

2. All the players close their eyes while the Game Master puts all the objects out on the table or floor and covers them with the towel.

3. All the players open their eyes. The Game Master picks up the towel and everyone has 2 minutes to memorize all the items.

4. After 2 minutes, the Game Master covers the objects with the towel, and each player writes down all the objects he or she can remember.

5. Then the Game Master uncovers the objects and the players can find out how they did.

How many of the 20 things did you remember? How did your friends do?

MEMORY SOLITAIRE

If you're not having a party, you can still test your memory with "Memory Solitaire."

WHAT DO I NEED?
• A timer, or a clock with a second hand and someone to tell you when 2 minutes are up
• A piece of paper and a pencil

WHAT DO I DO?

1. On page 16, there are pictures of 20 different things. To play, set the timer for 2 minutes (or have your friend tell you when to start). Then turn the page, and look at the pictures for 2 minutes.

2. When the time is up, close the book and write down as many of the things as you can remember. Ready, set, GO!

3. After you've written down as many as you can remember, open the book and check your list. How many of the 20 things did you remember?

IMPROVING YOUR MEMORY

Maybe you think you'll get better at memorizing things if you practice a lot. Sorry, but it doesn't work that way.

Back in 1927, a scientist tested 187 university students on their ability to memorize poetry, the meaning of Turkish words, dates of historical events, and other things.

Then some students practiced memorizing things. Others learned techniques for remembering things. And the rest did nothing at all related to memory.

When the scientist tested the students again, the group that had learned techniques for memorizing things did much better on the test than the others. The students who had practiced memorizing things and the students who had done nothing at all did about the same on the test as they did before.

Scientists have discovered that you don't get better at memorizing things just by doing it more. But you can get better by learning some clever tricks that help you out. We'll give you a few tricks you can try. They'll help you remember—and they'll also tell you something about how your memory works.

WORKING WITH YOUR WORKING MEMORY

Think about how you tried to remember the objects in one of the memory games. Some people try to remember them just by repeating them over and over, like this: comb, book, can of beans, left shoe, and so on. If you tried that, you were using what scientists call your "working memory."

When you look up a telephone number and repeat it over and over until you dial it, you're using your working memory. Your working memory is great for jobs like remembering a phone number for a few minutes.

Your working memory can hold a small amount of information for a relatively short time. Repeating a list of things over and over lets you remember some of the items on the list for a little while. But it's tough to store 20 different things in your working memory and remember them long enough to write them down.

To remember more things and to remember things longer, you want to transfer them from your working memory to your "long-term memory." Long-term memory is just what it sounds like, memories that last for a long time—days or months or years.

You can move things from working memory to long-term memory by making the stuff you are trying to remember meaningful in some way. The next 2 experiments show you 2 ways to put a list into your long-term memory. Try them out, and see how you do.

TELL YOURSELF A STORY

Use this trick to remember a list longer.

WHAT DO I NEED? • A timer, or a clock with a second hand and someone to tell you when two minutes are up
• A piece of paper and a pencil

WHAT DO I DO? **1.** On page 17, there are pictures of 20 different things. You are going to turn to the page, look at the pictures for 2 minutes, then close the book and write down as many of the things as you can remember.

2. While you are looking at the pictures, make up a story that has all those things in it. If you were looking at the pictures on page 16, you might make up a story about a man named Mr. Apple who wanted to gather a basket of bananas so he could make a banana cake. He stood on a chair and used a broom to knock bananas out of the tree. The chair tipped and he fell right into a cactus. Ouch! He got out the Band-Aids and . . .

3. You get the idea. If the story is silly, that's just fine. Try to imagine the story as you tell it to yourself, picturing Mr. Apple on the chair with the broom.

4. OK, now turn to page 17, look at the pictures, and make up your own story.

5. Are your 2 minutes up? Try to remember the pictures by telling yourself the story. You don't have to write down the story—just write down the things that it helps you remember.

How did you do!

When you tell yourself a story and imagine what's happening, you are doing a couple of things.

First, you are connecting the different pictures so that when you remember one, you remember the others, too. If you remember "Mr. Apple," you have a good chance of remembering "banana" and "cake" and "broom" and "chair" and "cactus." It's hard to remember all the items in a list where nothing is connected to anything else. It's easier to remember when one item is attached to a whole lot of others.

banana

cake

Mr. Apple

broom

Second, you are making a mental picture that includes all these different things. Making a mental picture helps you remember something later.

You may have discovered that making up a story didn't help you remember all the objects—but it helped you remember some of the objects for a lot longer. When you made a mental picture of the objects, you used your long-term memory, and that picture stuck with you.

WANDER AROUND YOUR HOUSE

This experiment is a great way to remember a list of things for a long time. Since it's a little harder than the last experiment, we decided to start small and remember 10 different things, rather than 20.

WHAT DO I NEED? • A familiar place to walk around—like your house
• A piece of paper and a pencil
• A timer, or a clock with a second hand and someone to tell you when 2 minutes are up

WHAT DO I DO? **1.** Walk through your house and write down a list of 10 different places where you could put something. For instance, you could put something on the couch in the living room, on top of the TV set, on the counter in the kitchen, and so on.

2. Spend a little bit of time imagining yourself walking from one place to another, looking at each place. Make sure that you can walk from one place to the next easily and in the same order every time.

3. Now you're going to turn to page 17 and look at the pictures for 2 minutes. Spend at least 8 seconds imagining each object in one of the places in your house. For instance, suppose one of the pictures was a duck and the bathtub was one of the places on your list. Imagine a duck doing the backstroke in the bathtub, surrounded by bubbles. The sillier the picture, the more likely you are to remember it.

4. Do the same thing for every item on the list.

5. When time is up, close the book and imagine yourself wandering through the house and looking in each of your places. Try to imagine the objects you put there. Write down all the objects you remember.

HOW DID YOU DO?

DID YOU REMEMBER ALL 10?

WHAT'S GOING ON? Sometimes all you need to help you remember something is a little hint. When you think "bathtub," that tells you to remember "duck" (or whatever you put in your bathtub).

This memory trick was invented after a grisly event in ancient Greece. Back in around 500 B.C., a Greek who won a wrestling match in the Olympic games celebrated by having a feast at his house. A man named Simonides gave a speech praising the wrestler, then he left the banquet hall. While he was out, the roof collapsed, crushing everyone inside. Though the bodies of the guests were mangled beyond recognition, Simonides could remember where each person had been seated. By doing that, he could name all of the people who were at the feast. Knowing where each person was sitting helped him remember who was there.

Any time you need to remember a list, you can use the same set of places in your house. One warning: When you remember a new list using the same places, you usually wipe out the old list. So if you need to remember more than one list, you need to have more than one set of places.

Ah ha! Simonides realized that he could use his imagination and a set of locations to help him remember other things. The trick you just learned is the same as Simonides's trick—but you used places in your house instead of seats at a banquet table.

SO WHAT?

You can apply these techniques to whatever you want to remember. Suppose you need to buy these 10 things at the store:

You could make up a story about how you wrapped toilet paper around your head because someone was going to be dropping tomatoes from the balcony. You tucked pieces of bread into the toilet paper turban to attract birds out of the apple tree. And so on, until you have a silly story that has all the things on the list in it. Or you could use your imagination to put these things all over your house, as you did in the "Wander Around Your House" trick.

Try these tricks when you've got to remember a list of things—whether it's stuff you need to buy at the store or vocabulary words for school—and see how your memory improves.

1) TOILET PAPER	6) CORNFLAKES
2) TOMATOES	7) MILK
3) A LOAF OF BREAD	8) LAUNDRY DETERGENT
4) APPLES	9) A CANDY BAR
5) HAMBURGER BUNS	10) CAT FOOD

WHAT NOW? If you want to try some other ways to improve your memory, check out "Get Organized" in the **Lost and Found** on page 23.

If you want to get better at remembering numbers, visit **Combination Cave** on page 26.

If you want to learn some other memory tricks, go to **Treasure Chest** on page 34.

If you want to try some puzzles that will stretch your memory, visit the **Logic Lounge** on page 110.

If you want to continue on in the **Caverns of Memory,** turn the page.

Memory Solitaire

Tell Yourself a Story

Wander Around Your House

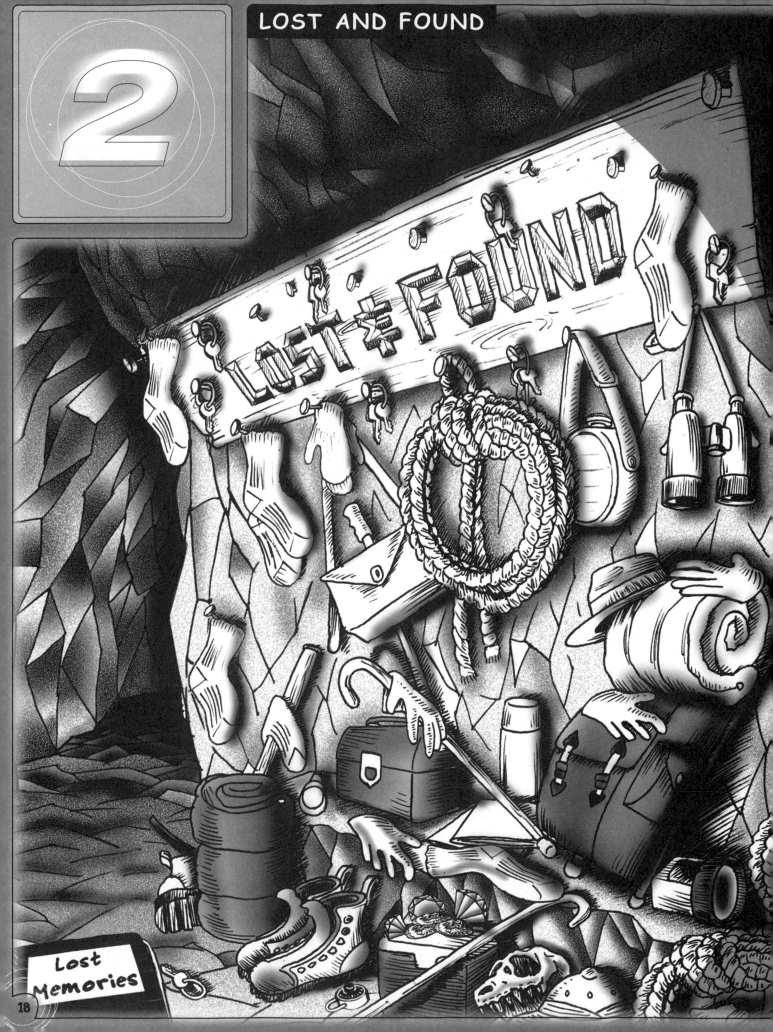

2

LOST MEMORIES

You depend on your brain to remember—but sometimes the information you need just doesn't seem to be there when you need it. You see a kid you used to play with and you can't remember his name. You study for a test, reading the things you are supposed to learn over and over again. But when you take the test, half of the information isn't there. Your brain has played a nasty trick on you and misplaced the memories you want.

Even remembering simple things can be a very tricky business. Playing with your tricky memory may help you figure out ways to keep it from letting you down—or at least help you understand why it does sometimes.

COMMON CENTS

You know exactly what a penny looks like, right? Maybe not.

WHAT DO I DO? Take a look at these pennies. Only one of these drawings of a penny is correct. Which one is it?

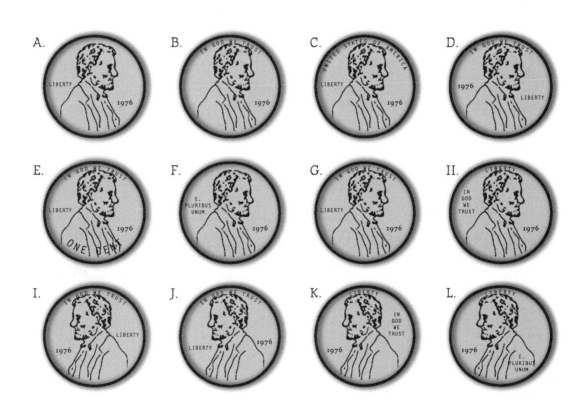

HOW DID YOU DO?   Go get a real penny and see if you picked the right drawing. (If you don't have a penny, the answer is on page 132.)

If you had a hard time choosing the right penny, you're not alone. If you're like most people, you don't have any trouble telling a penny from a dime or a nickel—but you don't have a very good memory for all the things that are on a penny.

Nobody knows exactly why people have trouble remembering or recognizing the details on pennies or other familiar objects. One theory is that people remember only enough about an object to let them recognize it in everyday life. Unless you collect pennies, you probably don't pay attention to details like the date or the words. Those details aren't important to you. You don't need them to tell an American penny from a dime, a nickel, or even a Canadian penny. If you get a copper coin with a picture of Lincoln on it, you figure it's an American penny.

The first step in remembering anything is to pay attention to it. Sometimes, when you think you've forgotten something, you never really knew it in the first place. The words on a penny may be like that. Chances are you never paid much attention to them before.

MIRROR IMAGES

When psychologists ask people to pick out the right penny from the possibilities, many people aren't sure whether Lincoln's head faces to the left or to the right. Apparently, your memory has difficulty telling the difference between a familiar object and its mirror image.

LOST SONGS

To show you how memories get lost, we need to help you misplace one. You'll need a friend to help you with this experiment.

WHAT DO I DO?   **1.** Think of song that you know by heart.

2. Ask your friend to start singing a different song—like "Twinkle, Twinkle, Little Star" or "Happy Birthday to You." While your friend is singing, try to recite (not sing) the words to your song.

WHAT'S GOING ON?   You probably had a hard time remembering the words to one song when your friend was singing another one. Most people do.

You remember the words to a song most easily when the right tune is playing. If there's no music, you can think of the tune and remember the words. But if someone's singing a different song, that tune and those words get in the way. You can't think of the tune or the words to the song you're trying to remember.

The Itsy-Bitsy Spider

Pop Goes the Weasel

The Star-Spangled Banner

Take me out to the Ball Game

I'm a Little Teapot

The ABC Song

TELLING YOUR BRAIN TO FETCH

The words to the song are stored in your brain. But when your friend is singing a different song, you have a hard time pulling those words back out of your brain.

Scientists call the process of pulling information out of your memory "retrieval." You think about something and your brain goes and brings that something back, like a dog retrieving a stick.

Each memory in your brain is connected to many other memories. A song's tune is linked to your memory of the song's words. Hearing the tune of a song can trigger your memory of the words, making them a lot easier to remember.

So if you can't remember the words to a song, try thinking of the tune. Or think about the last time you sang the song. Or think about when you learned the song. Those other memories may help you remember the words.

A IS FOR APPLE, B IS FOR CRAB

In this experiment, you'll look for some memories that are hard to find. Some clues help you remember a word—and others don't help much at all.

WHAT DO I DO? **1.** Get a piece of paper, a pencil, and a watch with a second hand. Use the watch to time yourself as you write down answers to the questions below.

HOW MANY OF THESE QUESTIONS CAN YOU ANSWER IN 2 MINUTES?

- What's a **fruit** beginning with the letter **P**?
  - What's an **animal** beginning with the letter **D**?
- What's a **metal** beginning with the letter **I**?
  - What's a **bird** beginning with the letter **B**?
- What's a **country** beginning with the letter **F**?
  - What's a **boy's name** beginning with the letter **H**?
- What's a **girl's name** beginning with the letter **P**?
  - What's a **vegetable** beginning with the letter **C**?
- What's a **sport** beginning with the letter **S**?
  - What's a **flower** beginning with the letter **P**?

Did you finish this list!

2. Now, here's another list of questions.

HOW MANY OF THESE QUESTIONS CAN YOU ANSWER IN 2 MINUTES?

- What's a **fruit** ending with the letter **H**?
- What's an **animal** ending with the letter **W**?
- What's a **metal** ending with the letter **R**?
- What's a **bird** ending with the letter **N**?
- What's a **country** ending with the letter **Y**?
- What's a **boy's name** ending with the letter **D**?
- What's a **girl's name** ending with the letter **N**?
- What's a **vegetable** ending with the letter **T**?
- What's a **sport** ending with the letter **L**?
- What's a **flower** ending with the letter **P**?

Did you finish this list, too!

Turn the page to see what's going on.

WHAT'S GOING ON? You probably wrote a lot of answers on the first list but had a much harder time with the second list. In both cases, you were asking your brain to fetch or retrieve a word it knows. You were giving your brain a clue about the word you wanted it to retrieve. Memory researchers call that a "retrieval cue." A retrieval cue helps you find where you stored a particular memory in your brain.

The letter that's at the beginning of the word is a good retrieval cue. Giving your brain the letter from the end of the word doesn't help you much at all. That suggests that your memory tends to organize words according to their beginning sounds, rather than their ending sounds. Of course, that's not the *only* way words are organized, or you wouldn't be able to name a fruit without running through the alphabet! If you got stumped for an answer to any of the questions, see page 132.

I'M THINKING OF...

Here are two tricks from the Lost and Found. Try them yourself, then use them to surprise your friends.

COLORFUL SURPRISE **1.** Think of a country that begins with the letter D.

2. Take the last letter in the name of the country and think of an animal that begins with *that* letter.

3. Now take the last letter in the name of the animal and think of a color that begins with *that* letter.

4. Go to page 132 and we'll tell you what color you're probably thinking of.

ADDING UP ANIMALS **1.** Think of a number between 1 and 10.

2. Multiply it by 9.

3. Take the number you get and add the digits together (If you got 18, add 1 + 8 to get 9.)

4. Subtract 5 from the number you get.

5. Count through the alphabet—saying A=1, B=2, C=3, and so on, until you reach your number.

D=4   **C=3**

6. Now think of a state that begins with the letter that matches your number.

7. Take the second letter of that state and think of an animal that begins with that letter. Turn to page 132 and we'll tell you what animal you're probably thinking of.

A=1

B=2

GET ORGANIZED!

Suppose you want to remember a list of words for school. Can visiting the Lost and Found help you with that? Sure it can. Try this.

WHAT DO I DO? **1.** Read these words out loud at a steady pace. Read them twice.

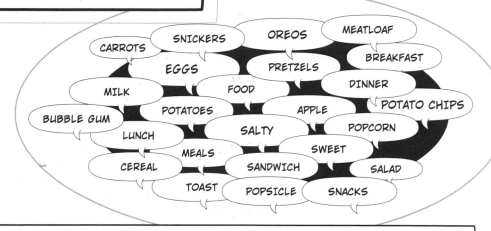

2. Now cover up the list and write down as many words as you can remember.

3. Look back at the list and see how you did. How many words did you remember? When you looked at the list, you probably thought, "Hey, I should have remembered *that* one!"

Now, you're going to try the same thing again with a different list of words.

1. Read all the words out loud at a steady pace. Read them twice.

ANIMALS

MAMMALS		OTHER		
Pets	Wild	Birds	Reptiles	Insects
dog	giraffe	crow	rattlesnake	ant
cat	zebra	eagle	horned toad	beetle
hamster	fox	ostrich	boa constrictor	termite
	elephant	peacock		

2. Cover up the list and write down as many words as you can remember.

WHAT'S GOING ON? Most people find it much easier to remember words in the list of animals. Why? In the first list, the words are not organized in any particular way. They all have something to do with food, but they are just a jumble of different food words.

In the second list, all the words have something to do with animals. But this time, the words are divided into groups with a heading above each group. "Animals" are divided into "mammals" and "other." "Mammals" are divided into "pets" and "wild." Scientists have found that people do a better job of remembering information that's subdivided and organized in this way.

Because the words in the second list are grouped under headings, you see the way they are connected to each other. If you think of one word, it's likely to make you think of a few of the others. If you think of the word "dog," for instance, you might think, "Oh, yeah. That was under 'pets.'"And when you think of "pets," you might also think of cats and hamsters. And that helps you remember the other words on the list.

WHAT ELSE CAN I DO? Try organizing the first list into groups. Does your organization make the words easier to remember? (If you want to find out how we organized these words, see page 132.)

Organizing information can help you out when you're trying to learn a list of words or facts. When you organize information, you create connections among the items in the list. When you remember one thing from the list, the connections will help your brain retrieve other things from the list.

REMEMBERING NAMES

One of the hardest things to remember (and one of the most embarrassing things to forget) is the name of a person you just met. How can you get better at remembering names?

WHAT DO I DO? Next time you meet someone new, try this.

1. Use the name right away. Say "Hi, Bob!" or Suzy or Joe or whatever the name is.

2. Imagine a picture that connects the name and face. Suppose you want to remember that a girl you just met is named Pat. Can you imagine someone patting Pat on her head?

WHY WILL THAT HELP? Lots of times you forget a name because you didn't really learn it in the first place. Step 1 makes sure you really listen to the name, because you need to use it right away. Saying the name helps, because when you want to remember the name, you are more likely to remember saying it than hearing it.

Names are hard to remember because nothing connects a name to a face. It's not as though everyone named Bob has brown hair or everyone named Susan has blue eyes. By imagining a connection, you help your memory out.

WHAT IF I FORGET THE NAME ANYWAY? Relax and think about something else. When you aren't trying anymore, the name may pop into your head. (Memory researchers call that a "pop-up.") Or try thinking about all the other things you know about the person: where they live, how you know them, where you met. Sometimes, pulling up all that information will pull up the name, too. You can also run through the alphabet. Sometimes, just thinking of the first letter will help you think of the whole name.

HOW CAN I KEEP MEMORIES FROM GETTING LOST?

You want your brain to fetch information you need, but sometimes your brain acts like a confused dog, unable to find the stick you just threw or the information that you just read. It isn't that your brain doesn't know the answer. It's just that it can't find the answer right now.

To make new memories easier to retrieve, you want to connect those memories to lots of other memories. You can do that by organizing new information so that it connects to stuff you already know or by thinking carefully about how things might link together.

You can think of memories as being like the strings in a fishing net. The more connections there are, the stronger the net will be. If the net is stronger, fewer sneaky memories will wiggle through the holes and escape, leaving you scratching your head and thinking, "I'm sure I know this—but I just can't remember."

WHAT NOW?

If you want to know how to remember numbers like a friend's phone number or your locker combination, go to **Combination Cave** on page 26.

If you've really lost something and want to find it, visit "Tricking Your Tricky Memory" in **Treasure Chest** on page 38.

If you liked the experiment called "A Is for Apple, B Is for Crab," go to the **Book of Beginnings** on page 120.

If you liked the experiment called "Get Organized," then challenge your ability to organize information in the **Logic Lounge** on page 110.

If you want to continue on in the **Caverns of Memory**, turn the page.

REMEMBERING NUMBERS

Some kids can remember 5 numbers in a row. Some can remember 10 in a row. Most people can remember 6 or 7 numbers in a row.

Who wants to remember numbers anyway? Well, some numbers are very handy to remember—like phone numbers and zip codes and the combination of the lock on the box full of batteries. (We're going to have to hurry to get out of the cave before our batteries run out!)

There are tricks that make remembering numbers easier. Try these out and see which ones work best for you.

CHUNKING

WHAT DO I DO? Read the numbers below out loud. Then cover them up and write down as many numbers as you can remember.

1 8 1 2 1 9 9 8 2 0 0 1

You probably read the numbers one by one, like this: 1, 8, 1, 2 . . . and so on. Now take a look at those numbers again and see if there's some other way you might have read them.

How did you do?

Instead of reading the numbers one by one, you can group them together to make 3 big numbers: 1812, 1998, and 2001. That way, you don't have to remember 12 different numbers—you just have to remember 3 big numbers.

You can use this trick with letters, too. Take a look at this row of letters. As you read it, group the letters into ways that make sense to you. Then cover up the row and see how many you remember.

T V F B I V C R C I A U S A N B C N A S A C B S R E M N Y P D

WHAT'S GOING ON? Scientists who study memory call this trick "chunking." Organizing lots of little things into larger chunks makes them easier to remember.

Without chunking, most people can remember between 5 and 9 numbers or letters. With chunking, many people can do much better. When you looked at the row of letters, some of the chunks you might have found are TV, FBI, and VCR. What other chunks can you find?

Here are some numbers that you can practice chunking with.

```
7 9 5 8 4 2 3
5 3 1 6 8 4 2
7 9 1 8 5 4 6
8 6 9 5 1 3 7 2
5 1 7 3 9 8 2 6
5 1 3 9 8 2 4 7
7 1 9 3 8 4 2 6 1
1 6 3 8 7 4 9 5 2
6 2 5 9 4 3 8 2 6
9 1 5 2 4 3 8 1 6 2
7 1 5 4 8 5 6 1 9 3
1 5 2 8 4 6 7 3 1 8
```

MAKING NUMBERS INTO WORDS

This is a great trick to use for numbers that you want to remember for a long time—like your best friend's phone number.

WHAT DO I DO? The push buttons on a telephone have letters on them as well as numbers. In San Francisco, you can find out what time it is by dialing 767-2676. Or you can dial POPCORN—the letters that are on the same buttons as those numbers.

You can match the letters and numbers on the phone to make words out of telephone numbers that you want to remember. On the right are the letters that go with each number.

Start with a phone number you want to remember. Write down the letters that go with each digit. Since one and zero don't have any letters, you need to be creative. You could use the letter I for one, as long as you remember to dial one instead of I (which goes with number 4). You could use the letter O for zero, as long as you remember you've done that. (The letter O is on the button with number 6.)

Now figure out a word that you can make by stringing together one of the letters that goes with each number.

For example, suppose you're in San Francisco and you want to remember the number of the Exploratorium's information line: 397-5673.

1 - no letters

2 - ABC

3 - DEF

4 - GHI

5 - JKL

6 - MNO

7 - PRS

8 - TUV

9 - WXY

0 - no letters

Let's see how the numbers match up with letters:

3	9	7	5	6	7	3
DEF	WXY	PRS	JKL	MNO	PRS	DEF

That translates into **EXPLORE,** an easy word to remember. Most phone numbers won't make that much sense. (The number for the Exploratorium's main switchboard, 563-7337, becomes JOE-REDS.) Even words that don't make a lot of sense are easier to remember than a bunch of numbers.

Try to make a word out of your phone number or the phone number of a friend.

LOOKING FOR MEANING

If a phone number you are trying to remember doesn't make a word, try this trick.

Some people look at the digits in a phone number and try to figure out how they relate to each other. For instance, suppose you want to remember the number 459-8412.

You might say that 4 + 5 = 9 and 8 + 4 = 12. That could help you remember.

Take a phone number you want to remember and see if the numbers relate to each other in some way that makes them memorable.

$$4 + 5 = 9 \text{ and } 8 + 4 = 12$$

WHAT NOW? If you liked making words from phone numbers, go to **Leak Lake** on page 54.

If you want to continue on in the **Caverns of Memory,** just turn the page.

DROODLES

A droodle is a combination of a doodle and a riddle. Playing with these droodles lets you exercise your memory and your creativity—and will help you discover what makes some things easier to remember than others.

NONSENSE DROODLES

WHAT DO I DO? Get a piece of paper and a pencil. On your paper, draw four squares that are about the size of the squares on this page. Under each square, write one of these words: Cend, Rist, Blish, Teaf.

Now spend a few moments looking at the four droodles on this page. Try to remember each droodle and the word that goes with it. Then turn the page.

Blish

Cend

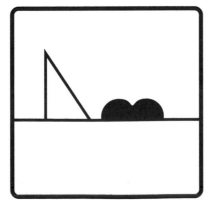

Rist

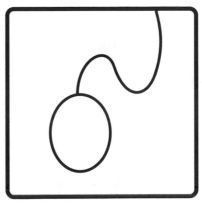

Teaf

Now, on your piece of paper, try to draw the droodle that goes with each word. This is a memory test—no fair going back to look at the pictures!

How did you do?
  Turn to the previous page to check your answers.

DROODLES WITH NAMES

WHAT DO I **DO?** On a piece of paper, draw 4 squares. Under each square, write one of these phrases:

A waffle that an elephant stepped on   Fried egg, sunny-side down

Ship arriving too late to save a drowning witch   Inchworm on roller skates

Now take a look at these droodles. Try to memorize the droodle that goes with each title. Then close the book and try to draw the picture that goes with each phrase.

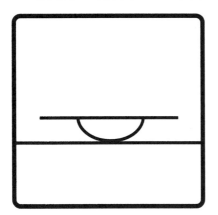

Fried egg, sunny-side down

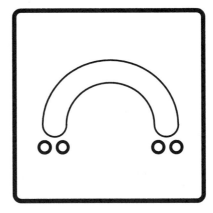

Inchworm on roller skates

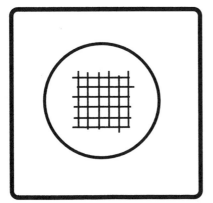

A waffle that an
elephant stepped on

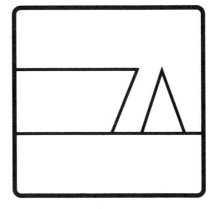

Ship arriving too late
to save a drowning witch

Did you draw all four pictures?
Did you have better luck with these than you did with the first set of droodles?

WHAT'S GOING ON? If you're like most people, you found it was easier to remember the droodles when the title made the picture into a joke. Without these titles, the droodles are just meaningless squiggles. Memorizing meaningless stuff is hard. And giving meaningless squiggles nonsense titles like "Teaf" and "Rist" doesn't make them any easier to remember! (See page 132 for meaningful titles for those first four droodles.)

Teaf

Rist

It's easiest to remember stuff that makes sense to you and connects with other stuff you know. The droodle labeled "Ship arriving too late to save a drowning witch" is pretty silly, but it does fit with things you know. You know witches wear pointy hats. You know what a side view of a ship on the water looks like. Knowing these things helps you make sense of the picture and remember it better.

Blish

Cend

WHAT ELSE CAN I DO? Try coming up with a memorable title for this droodle.

What do you think this is?

Try drawing your own droodles and giving them titles.

The person who drew it says that it's an elephant on roller blades. Another person guessed that it's 3 nearsighted bald men watching TV. There really isn't one right answer. In fact, if you come up with a funny answer that you like a lot, you're more likely to remember the droodle.

WHAT NOW?

If you'd like to play with other pictures that are riddles, go to the **Plexer Studio** on page 92.

If you'd like to play with puzzles that make pictures, check out the **Temple of Tan** on page 82.

If you like cartoons, visit **Moonstruck on the Mountain** on page 42.

If you like coming up with many names for the same droodle, visit the **Playroom** on page 124.

If you want to continue to explore the **Caverns of Memory,** just turn the page.

YOUR TRICKY MEMORY

Have you ever gotten into an argument with a friend about something that you remember? He says you went to the movies on Friday and you say that you went on Saturday. And you get into a big fight because you can't agree.

Who's right? That's hard to say, unless you can find some other way to figure out what happened. Maybe you could find the stub of your movie ticket. Strange though it may seem, you can't always trust your memory.

Memory researchers have discovered that things you see or hear after an event can change your memory of what happened. Here are some experiments that will show you how tricky your memory can be, and a few tricks that will help you outsmart your tricky memory.

A VERY BAD DAY

Read the following story.

John got to class just as Mr. Smith was walking up and down between the desks, handing each kid a piece of paper. "I hope you all did your homework last night," Mr. Smith was saying. "This quiz will be an important part of your grade. Keep your eyes on your own paper and get to work." John stared at the problems. He hadn't done his homework and he was doing badly in this class to begin with. He guessed at one answer and wrote it down, then thought some more and erased it. Desperate, he looked up at the clock to see how much time was left. Sitting at the desk right in front of him was the smartest girl in the class. He saw some of her answers and wrote them down. He looked up again and saw Mr. Smith staring right at him. He knew he was in big trouble.

1. Now cover up the story.

2. Without looking back, pick the words below that appeared in the story:

3. Now uncover the paragraph and check your answers.

STUDENT	SCHOOL	QUIZ	SCARED	PENCIL
TEACHER	CLASS	CHEAT	NERVOUS	HOMEWORK

Turn the page to learn what's going on.

WHAT'S GOING ON? When you read a story like the one on page 35, you tend to think about where it's happening—and that makes the story easier to understand. In this story, you probably figured out that John was a student at school. Once you figured that out, it was easier to make sense of the story.

But figuring that out may also have made you remember words that weren't there—words you would expect to see in a story about a student at school taking a test. Most people think the words "student" and "teacher" and "cheat" are in the story, but they aren't. The words "quiz," "class," and "homework" were in the story, but none of the other words on the list are in the story!

PHANTOM WORDS

Here's an experiment to try with a friend. It's also a great experiment to try on a grown-up.

WHAT DO I DO? **1.** Don't let your friend look at this list.

2. Say this to your friend: "I'm going to read you a list of 30 words. Then I'll read a few more words and ask you if you remember them from the list. The important thing isn't how many words you remember. The important thing is *which* words they are."

3. Read these words to your friend:

sour	nice	pin	bitter
thread	point	heart	chocolate
eye	thorn	injection	sharp
candy	hurt	cake	good
syringe	honey	tart	prick
sugar	thimble	pie	taste
haystack	cloth	knitting	tooth
sewing	soda		

4. Now ask your friend if he or she remembers these words:

candy (Yes, it was on the list.)   eye (Yes, it was on the list.)
bread (No, it wasn't on the list.)   lamp (No, it wasn't on the list.)
sweet (No, it wasn't on the list.)   needle (No, it wasn't on the list.)

WHAT'S GOING ON? After hearing the list, most people think that they heard the words "sweet" and "needle," even though they didn't hear those words.

Memory works by linking different thoughts together. A thought about one thing can trigger a related thought about something else. The first list has lots of words that are linked to the word "sweet." It includes many words for sweet things (like candy and cake) and some words that are linked to "sweet." "Heart," for example, might make you think of the word "sweetheart." Because your brain kept thinking about "sweet," you may remember that word as being on the list.

WHAT IF I WANT TO TRY IT AGAIN? If you want to try it again, here's another list of words to use.

mad	wrath	calm	bike	fear
happy	plain	temper	hill	climb
range	fury	hate	fight	emotion
molehill	rage	valley	climber	ire
glacier	summit	enrage	steep	hatred
mean	ski	peak	goat	top

Now ask your friend if he or she remembers these words:

fury (Yes, it was on the list.)
chair (No, it wasn't on the list.)
anger (No, it wasn't on the list.)
valley (Yes, it was on the list.)
apple (No, it wasn't on the list.)
mountain (No, it wasn't on the list.)

After hearing this list, most people think they heard the words "anger" and "mountain," even though those words aren't on the list.

TRICKING YOUR TRICKY MEMORY

Sometimes, all it takes for you to remember something is a little clue. Here are a few ways people jog their memories.

IF YOU WANT TO REMEMBER TO DO SOMETHING...

Write yourself a reminder on a list or on a calendar—or on your hand. One of the members of the Science-at-Home team writes all the things she has to remember on her hand. It's easier to explain why she has "cookies" written on her hand than to explain to the other members of the team that she left the cookies back at Base Camp.

IF YOU'VE LOST SOMETHING... You may be able to remember where you left it by thinking about where you've been—step by step. If thinking about where you've been doesn't help, try going to the places you might have left it. Sometimes, being there will jog your memory.

TO REMEMBER ALL THE COLORS IN THE RAINBOW... Remember the name ROY G. BIV. Each letter in the name stands for a color: Red, Orange, Yellow, Green, Blue, Indigo, Violet. (Red is on the outside of the rainbow's curve and violet is on the inside.)

TO REMEMBER THE PLANETS IN THE SOLAR SYSTEM... Use the sentence "Mother Very Early Made A Jelly Sandwich Using No Peanuts." If you take the first letter of each word, you get the first letter of each planet (and the Asteroid Belt) as you move away from the sun. (Mercury, Venus, Earth, Mars, Asteroid Belt, Jupiter, Saturn, Uranus, Neptune, Pluto.)

TO REMEMBER HOW TO SPELL TRICKY WORDS... To remember that dessert (like ice cream and cake) is spelled with a double S, tell yourself that dessert is so sweet (SS). To remember that desert (a place with very little water) is spelled with only one S, tell yourself that a desert is so dry (S).

You write a letter on stationery. You are stationary when you aren't moving. How can you remember to spell one with "ar" and one with "er"? You can remember that you write a lettER on stationery. And you can remember that stationary is when you ARen't moving.

Sometimes rhymes can help you remember spelling rules.

I before E except after C

Or when sounding like A as in neighbor and weigh.

Either, neither, weird, and seize

are four exceptions, if you please.

TO REMEMBER HOW MANY DAYS ARE IN A MONTH...

In English, we have a rhyme that helps:
Thirty days hath September, April, June, and November.
All the rest have thirty-one, excepting February alone,
And that has twenty-eight days clear
And twenty-nine in each leap year.

People in Italy, France, and the Netherlands have similar rhymes in their own languages. In Greece, Finland, Russia, China, Tibet, and most of South America, people use a method of counting on their knuckles. Make a fist and count off the months, using your knuckles and the valleys between the knuckles. January is on a knuckle, so it's long; February is in a valley, so it's short. March is long; April is short; May is long; June short; July long. Then you run out of knuckles, so you start again at the beginning with a knuckle. August is long, September is short, and so on.

January
February
March
April
May June July
August
September
October
November
December

TO REMEMBER HOW TO MULTIPLY BY 9...

Having a hard time remembering what you get when you multiply 9 times any number from 1 to 9? Here's a trick that helps.

Hold out your two hands with the palm side up. Decide what you want to multiply by 9. Starting with your left thumb, count over that many fingers and fold that finger down. Now, all the fingers to the left are 10 and all the fingers to the right are ones.

So if you want to multiply 9 times 3, fold down your third finger. There are 2 fingers to the left, so that's 20. There are 7 fingers to the right, so that's 7. The answer is 27!

Works every time.

1	9
2	18
3	27
4	36
5	45
6	54
7	63
8	72
9	81
10	90

$\times 9 =$

WHAT NOW?

If you want to try some tricky puzzles, check out **Through the Trapdoor** on page 98.

If you want to continue on into the **Forest of Hidden Surprises,** just turn the page.

FOREST OF HIDDEN SURPRISES

You step out of the Caverns of Memory and find yourself halfway up a mountain. You follow a path downward through some very strange places. To explore these places, turn to the page numbers shown.

WHY IS THERE A MAN IN THE MOON?

ABOUT FACES

1

MOONSTRUCK ON THE MOUNTAIN PAGE 42

WHAT'S WITH ALL THESE GAPS, ANYWAY?

Filling in the Blanks

2

JUMPING THE GAP PAGE 48

MIX UP THE LETTERS IN "LEAK" AND YOU GET "LAKE." WHAT'S GOING ON HERE?

OBOE KNOT NOTEBOOK

3

LEAK LAKE PAGE 54

4

GROTTO OF GAMES PAGE 60

5

TRICKERY THICKET PAGE 68

6

GARDEN OF ILLUSIONS PAGE 76

As you step away from the Temple of Tan, you see a strange building high in the trees ahead. To explore the Puzzle House, go to page 90.

7

TEMPLE OF TAN PAGE 82

ABOUT FACES

If you show a baby these three pictures, chances are the kid will like the middle one best.

That's because it looks kind of like a human face, with two eyes above a mouth.

People are born knowing how to recognize other human faces. Because of this basic instinct for recognizing faces, people tend to see a face in any pattern that has spots and lines that look a little bit like two eyes and a mouth—like the face of the Man in the Moon.

People are also very good at figuring out how people feel from the expressions on their faces. Anthropologists have discovered that people all over the world share the same facial expressions for basic emotions.

You know that one of these guys is angry and one is sad—and you know which is which.

FACES IN THE FUNNIES

Take a look at the comics in your local newspaper. Even though some characters' faces are just a lot of squiggles, you still recognize Charlie Brown. You can even tell what he's feeling by the arrangement of his squiggles.

WHAT DO I NEED? • A newspaper comics page
• Scissors
• Plain paper

WHAT DO I DO? Cut out as many faces as you want from the comics page. Take a good look at the lines and dots that make up each face. Do all of the characters have complete faces—two eyes and eyebrows, a nose, and a mouth?

Use a piece of plain paper to cover up part of each face. Ask a friend if he can identify who the cartoon character is. Is it easier to recognize the more realistic characters? Chances are it won't take much information—just a few lines—for him to identify any character.

Turn the page to learn what's going on.

WHAT'S GOING ON? Even if they're drawing animals or space creatures, cartoonists draw their characters to form patterns that suggest human faces and emotions. That makes the cartoon much more appealing to you, the human reader. But if you look carefully, you may also discover that your favorite cartoon character doesn't have a nose (or a mouth, or eyebrows)—and you never noticed that before. Your brain doesn't need a complete pattern to recognize a face.

EMOTICONS OR SMILEYS

Use punctuation to let people know what you're feeling.

WHAT DO I DO? Take a look at this strange punctuation. :) It's a colon, followed by the right half of a set of parentheses. Now turn your head sideways. It looks like a smiling face. When people are talking by computer e-mail, they sometimes let their friends know they are joking by ending a sentence with a "smiley" like that one.

A smiley (also called an "emoticon") is a cartoon made only of punctuation marks. When people started communicating with e-mail, they developed smileys to express their feelings using symbols on the keyboard.

Here are a few smileys. Match them with their descriptions.

8)	**Person sticking out tongue**
:-O	**Abraham Lincoln**
=I:-)=	**Surprised person**
;-)	**Marge Simpson**
:-P	**Person winking**
****:-)	**Person wearing glasses**

See page 133 for solutions.

If you have a computer or typewriter, try making up your own smileys!

FLIP-A-FACE

Most of the faces you see are right-side up. When a face is upside down, it's harder for your brain to recognize it as a face, because the pattern is wrong—the eyes are at the bottom and the mouth is at the top.

WHAT DO I NEED? • A full-page color photograph of a face. You can cut one out of an ad in a fashion magazine. Or you can use a color copy of a photo of your own face (or your brother or sister's face). *Don't* cut up a photograph; use a copy!

• Scissors

• Tape

Don't cut up a photograph; USE A COPY!

WHAT DO I DO? **1.** Start with a full-page photo of a face.

2. Cut out three rectangles—one around the mouth and one around each eye. Make sure to include some skin around each eye and the mouth.

3. Turn the magazine page over so that you're looking at the back. Turn over all three rectangles so that you're looking at the back of those.

4. Turn each rectangle upside down and put it back into the hole you cut it out of. Tape all three upside-down rectangles in place.

5. When all three rectangles are taped, turn the whole page upside down. Now turn the page over so that you're looking at the front again.

6. Look at the face. It should be upside down. Do you see a smile? How do the eyes look?

7. Now turn the page right-side up and look at the face. Arghh! It's a monster!

WHAT'S GOING ON? When the picture is upside down, your brain has to work hard to recognize it as a face to begin with. So you aren't really paying attention to details. You don't notice that the eyes and the mouth don't match the rest of the face. But that becomes *very* obvious as soon as you turn the picture right-side up.

FINDING FACES EVERYWHERE

The world's a really messy and complicated place. Your brain tries to make sense of all the stuff you see around you—and that's not an easy thing to do.

Sometimes, when your brain is trying to figure out what's out there, you remember what you've seen before and try to match that with what you're seeing now. Your brain may take a shortcut and say, "Hey, this looks kind of like something I've seen before. I guess that's what it is!"

The dark patches on the moon look kind of like a face, so your brain sees a face. A face is what scientists call a "preferred pattern" for your brain—you can't help seeing faces. It's so basic to the way your brain makes sense of the world that you've probably seen "faces" everywhere— in clouds, in the bark of trees, even on cars and buildings.

TREES

CARS

BUILDINGS

WHAT DO I DO? Go for a walk around your house or your neighborhood, and see how many faces you can find. (The ones on the fronts of people's heads don't count!) Look for dials, headlights, nails, and screws that look like eyes. Look for holes that look like surprised mouths, or curves that look like smiles or frowns. On the right are some faces that photographers have found.

WHAT NOW?

If you want to experiment with other visual patterns, check out the **Plexer Studio** on page 92 or **A Shift at the Snack Bar** on page 102.

If you want to experiment with your memory for pictures, visit **Base Camp** on page 10 or **Cave Paintings** on page 30.

If you want to discover other ways that what you expect determines what you see, go to the **Garden of Illusions** on page 76.

If you want to continue to explore the **Forest of Hidden Surprises,** turn the page.

2

Filling in
the Blanks

FILLING IN THE BLANKS

Read the poem below and try to fill in the missing words.

Mary had a little _____
Whose fleece was _____ as snow,
And everywhere that _____ went
The _____ was sure to _____.

That was probably pretty easy. You read the first line, remembered a familiar poem, and filled in the gaps where words were missing.

This is an example of a place where your brain sees a blank and fills it in. You recognize something familiar and use what you remember to fill in the blank.

Your brain is always looking for blank spaces and filling them in. Usually, you don't notice what's going on. But sometimes your brain leaps to the wrong conclusion and fills in a blank with the wrong answer. Then you get a surprise!

JUMPING TO CONCLUSIONS

Did you have to work really hard to learn how to read? Most people do. But after you've been reading for a few years, your brain gets really good at recognizing letters.

WHAT DO I DO? We've carefully covered these words so you can only see part of each letter. But try to read them anyway. What do you think they say?

JUMPING TO CONCLUSIONS

1. Turn to page 133 to check your answer. Chances are you thought you had enough information to read this message. But if you look at the answer, you'll find out that the answer you came up with wasn't the only one possible.

2. You only see part of each letter. Your brain compares this part to its memory of letters and tries to figure out what the covered up part might look like. Your brain looks for a pattern. What word could have all these letters? Then your brain fills in the missing pieces. Because your brain tries to make sense of the world, it completes the letters to produce familiar words.

3. After you check the answer, you may say, "But that doesn't make sense!" You're right. It's just a bunch of letters. Your brain read this collection of letters as "JUMPING TO CONCLUSIONS" because *that* makes sense.

49

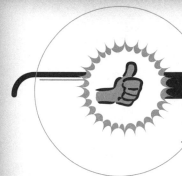

WHO GOES THERE?

Here's a way to fool your friends with the same trick that we just used to fool you.

WHAT DO I DO? **1.** If you have a computer or a typewriter, you can make your own confusing messages. Type out the alphabet, using all capital letters.

ABCDEFGHIJKLMNOPQRSTUVWXYZ

2. Use a piece of paper to cover up the bottom half of the alphabet. Which letters or numbers look like other letters or numbers when they are partly covered?

If you cover the bottom half,
C looks like G
E looks like F
H looks like U
I looks like J or L
R looks like P or B
O looks like Q
X looks like Y

3. Now take the letters in your name. See if you can make a collection of letters that look like your name when the bottom half is covered. Type those letters, then cover up the bottom half. Ask people if they can read the words—and see how many people you can fool.

Science-at-Home team member, Pat Murphy, created this version of her name.

PAT MURPHY

Remove the black bar and you get:

RAT MHPRUX

What can you do with your name?

THE TRIANGLE THAT ISN'T THERE

Take a look at these pictures. What do you see?

Most people see a bright triangle that stands out in front of all the other shapes on the paper.

Do you see a ghostly gray square lying on top of the circles?

WHAT'S GOING ON? **1.** In these pictures, you probably *see* familiar shapes: a triangle and a square. These shapes have no solid border or outline, but you see them anyway. The triangle and the square exist only in your mind. Your eyes and brain create them in an effort to make sense of the shapes on the page.

2. Look at the triangle again. This design is really three circles with slices taken out of them and three sets of lines that form arrowheads. But that's a complicated pattern of shapes. To make it simpler, your brain sees the picture as a collection of very familiar shapes—triangles and circles. To see the picture this way, your eyes and brain fill in some missing information, making a bright triangle even though there really isn't one.

WHAT ABOUT THAT SQUARE? The same thing is going on in the picture of the square. Your brain can either see a bunch of circles that are partly gray, or it can see a bunch of black circles with a ghostly gray square on top of them. The second explanation is simpler, so that's what you see.

WHY DOES YOUR BRAIN DO THIS? Your brain has to work hard to make sense of the world. So sometimes it takes a shortcut. Seeing the shapes that aren't there is a mental shortcut—it lets your brain quickly sort through some strange-looking pictures.

Do you see a curved line running through these horizontal lines?

HANGMAN

Here's a game to play with a friend. Fill in the blanks, guess the right word, and save yourself from getting hanged!

WHAT DO I DO?

1. Have your friend think of a word and draw the hangman's gallows (the picture that's labeled "start"). Have your friend draw one blank space for each letter in the word.

2. Now you guess a letter. If that letter is part of the word, your friend fills in any blank space (or spaces) where that letter goes. If the letter is *not* part of the word, your friend draws your head in the gallows.

3. Now guess another letter. Every time you guess right, your friend fills in a blank. But every time you guess wrong, your friend adds another body part to your hanging body. The game ends when you guess the word, or when you've had 6 wrong guesses, and you are hanged.

You and your friend can switch roles after each game, or play a few games and then switch.

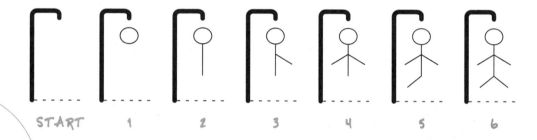

START   1   2   3   4   5   6

HOW TO MAKE GOOD GUESSES

GUESS A VOWEL FIRST

Every word in the English language contains at least one vowel. There are only 6 vowels (A E I O U and Y). The letter E is the most common vowel. The letter Y is kind of an oddball, because it is sometimes used as a vowel (as in the word "why") and sometimes as a consonant (as in the word "yellow").

A long word may have 2 or even 3 different vowels, so guess until you get a couple of them. But if the word is short (4 or 5 letters), you're better off getting one vowel, and then moving on to consonants.

GUESS COMMON LETTERS

Some letters (like E and I) appear in lots of words in the English language, and some (like Q and J) are only in a few. Here's one researcher's idea of how the alphabet would look if all the letters were listed in the order of how often they're used:

After you've filled in some blanks with vowels, start guessing common consonants.

E I A O R N T S L C U P M D H Y G B F U K W Z X Q T

HOW TO STUMP YOUR FRIEND

• Don't pick a word that only has very common letters.

• If you use a very short word with a common vowel, make sure it has less-common consonants. (Words like "deem," "fizz," or "jaunt" are good.)

• Short words with uncommon letters make really good stumpers ("crypt" is a great one).

• Use unusual words—like "graphic" or "azure." But no fair using words your friend's never heard of!

WHEEL OF FORTUNE

Have you ever watched the TV show Wheel of Fortune? *It's basically the same game as Hangman, with a few differences: They don't use a gallows, they spin a wheel to see how much money each guess is worth, and you have to buy a vowel. Oh yes, and on Wheel of Fortune, the letter* y *is always considered a consonant, not a vowel.*

OTHER WAYS TO PLAY HANGMAN

• Give the guesser more chances by adding details to the hanging person. (Giving it hands and feet adds 4 more guesses.)

• Use phrases, titles, or names instead of single words. Leave extra space between the blanks of one word and the blanks of another.

• Play with categories—cities, presidents, astronomy, food, cartoons, movies, etc. This gives the guesser an extra clue about what the word (or words) might be.

• Use a watch or clock to play a timed version, with points, but no hanging person. Guess as many times as you want. But each second of time counts as one point, and each wrong guess is 5 points. Play 5 words, then switch roles. The person with the lowest score wins.

SO WHAT?

You may not need very many letters for your brain to recognize a word or phrase. Your brain is really good at filling in the blanks. It has to be. The information that your brain gets about the world is incomplete—so your brain has to guess to make a whole picture.

When your brain fills in a blank, it makes a guess based on what you've seen before. Your memory of what the world is like tells your brain what to expect—and that helps your brain make a good guess.

WHAT NOW?

If you liked playing Hangman because you like playing with words, visit **Leak Lake** on page 54 or the **Book of Beginnings** on page 120 or "A Is for Apple, B is for Crab" in the **Lost and Found** on page 21.

If you liked playing Hangman because you like playing games with a friend, go to **Grotto of Games** on page 60.

If you want to continue to *explore* the **Forest of Hidden Surprises**, turn the page.

OBOE KNOT NOTEBOOK

Take a look at the words "oboe knot" and the word "notebook." Do you see something that they have in common?

The letters in "notebook" can be rearranged to make "oboe knot." Words like this are called *anagrams.* You can make a basic anagram by rearranging the letters of one word to make another word or words—"leak" becomes "lake." You can use the letters in "grassland" to make "darn glass." "Grotto" makes "go trot."

Here on the shores of Leak Lake, the Science-at-Home team started playing games with anagrams and had a lot of fun.

Did you know that you can rearrange the letters in "a lot of fun" to get "ant off lou" or "flaunt foo," which doesn't make much sense but is fun to say.

PLAYING ANAGRAM GAMES

How many little words can you make from a bigger word?

WHAT DO I DO? **1.** Get a piece of paper and a pencil and a watch.

2. Choose one of the words to the right. Give yourself 10 minutes and see how many different words you can make out of that word. Try making 3-letter words, 4-letter words, and even longer words, if you can.

pirates

substitute

magazine

computer

adventure

3. There's not just one right answer. There may be dozens, or even hundreds of different little words that you can make from a single word. Seeing how many different words you can think of is a good way to exercise your creativity. Creative people are good problem solvers because they don't stop when they've found one solution. They keep looking to see what else they might come up with.

4. If you feel stuck and can't think of any more little words, try some of the tips on page 56. One of them is sure to give your brain a little bit of a boost.

ANAGRAM PARTY GAME You can play this kind of anagram game with a group of people. Use one of the words above, or look in the dictionary for a word that's 7 to 10 letters long. Then give everyone 10 minutes to make a list of all the little words they can make out of that word. Give each person 1 point for every 3-letter word, 2 points for every 4-letter word, 3 points for every 5-letter word, and so on. You can also keep score by only awarding points for words that no one else thought of.

TIPS AND TRICKS

The Science-at-Home team has some tricks that help us make lots of little words from big words. To see how these tricks work, try to make as many words as you can from the letters in the word "information."

TRICK #1: ALPHABETICAL ORDER

Write out the letters in alphabetical order, and "information" becomes "a f i i m n n o o r t" When we did that, we suddenly saw the word "root," and that led us to a whole new list of words.

information

afiimnnoort

"root"

"fan" "tan" "man"

"ram" "rat"

"tram" "from"

TRICK #2: CHANGE THE CONSONANTS

Start with the word "ran" and replace the R with other consonants from "information." That makes "fan," "tan," and "man." Move to the other end of the word. Replace the N to get "ram" and "rat."

Play with pairs of consonants—like TR and FR at the beginning of a word. You'll get words like "ram," "tram," and "from." Use pairs of consonants—like RT and RN—at the end of a word to get "fort" and "torn."

TRICK #3: CHANGE THE VOWELS

Changing the vowel in a word may make a new word. "Tan" becomes "ton" or "tin." Use pairs of vowels to make words like "main," "root," or "fair."

"fort" "torn"

"ton" "tin"

"main" "root" "fair"

"ton" "not"

"room" "moor"

TRICK #4: GO BACKWARDS

Reverse the order of letters in a word to see if you get a new word. "Ton" becomes "not." "Room" becomes "moor."

TRICK #5: MIX AND MATCH

Put all these tricks together. When we put the letters in alphabetical order, "room" jumped out at us. We turned it around to make "moor" and started playing with the consonants and vowels. All of a sudden we had "moat," "moot," "root," "foot," and even "motor."

"room"

"moat" "moot" "root"

"foot" "motor"

A DORMITORY IS A DIRTY ROOM

Another way of playing with anagrams is to use all the letters in one word or phrase to make another word or phrase. "Berry Bush . . . Shrubbery" is like that.

Check out these anagrams. The second phrase tells you something about the first word or words. Here are some of our favorite examples.

astronomers	moonstarers
a decimal point	I'm a dot in place
Clint Eastwood	old west action
the active volcanos	cones evict hot lava
eleven + two	twelve + one

Here's another kind of anagram, sometimes called an "antigram." The second phrase tells you something that contradicts the original word or words.

earliest	rise late
forty five	over fifty
the ship Titanic	hasn't hit ice tip

SECRET MESSAGES

Galileo sometimes wrote his scientific discoveries down as anagrams, so that no one would steal his work before he was ready to publish it.

It's hard to take a word or phrase and come up with something that uses the same letters and relates to the first word. But it's not so hard to make anagrams that will make you laugh.

WHAT DO I DO? **1.** Start with the letters of your own name. You can use your first and last name, or add your middle name in, too.

2. If you have a Scrabble game, get a tile for each letter in your name. If you don't have Scrabble tiles, write each letter down on a piece of paper or a Post-it note. Then just start moving the pieces around, rearranging the letters, and see what words you can make. See if you can create a phrase that uses all the letters in your name.

The Science-at-Home team tried making anagrams of "science at home." Here are some of our favorites.

a Chinese comet

chaotic men see

moccasin, tee hee!

can echoes emit?

omit each scene

teach me ice, son

Inca emcee shot

rice oat scheme

octane chemise

PINKISH RIPPLE

Home Scientist Greg Perkins has a brother named Philip. They made an anagram of Philip's name. Instead of Philip Perkins, he's now know as "Pinkish Ripple." (Greg's mom, Diane Reese, is now called "Serene Idea.")

WHERE ELSE CAN I FIND ANAGRAMS?

If your family gets a daily newspaper, chances are there are one or two new word puzzles every day. Lots of newspapers print a feature called the "Jumble," which is a kind of anagram puzzle. Your paper may also run puzzles in the Sunday comics. If a puzzle is called something like "word scramble," it's probably a kind of anagram.

To combine playing with words and playing with other people, try some games like Scrabble and Boggle. They're played with a lot of the same skills you use when you make anagrams. The world is full of ways to play with words. Just keep your eyes peeled and your pencils sharpened.

LOOKING FOR PATTERNS

Playing with anagrams helps you start to see the patterns that letters form in the English language. You might notice, for instance, that you'll start to see what consonants appear together. At the beginning of a word, you'll see combinations like "st" or "ch," but never "ng." You'll see "ng" at the end of a word.

We should probably warn you about one thing. Once you start to notice patterns, you'll see them everywhere. If you have a good time playing with anagrams, you may find that you can't spell a word without noticing how the letters combine—and thinking about what anagrams it could make. ("Spell a word" could be "Alps red owl" or "a droll spew.")

WHAT NOW?

If you want more word puzzles, go to the **Book of Beginnings** on page 120, the **Plexer Studio** on page 92, or "One Word Answer" in **Through the Trapdoor** on page 99.

If you want to play another word game, check out "Hangman" in **Jumping the Gap** on page 52.

If you like scrambling up the pieces of something and seeing what else you can make, go to the **Temple of Tan** on page 82.

If you liked seeing unexpected connections, visit the **Playroom** on page 124.

If you want to continue to explore the **Forest of Hidden Surprises,** turn the page.

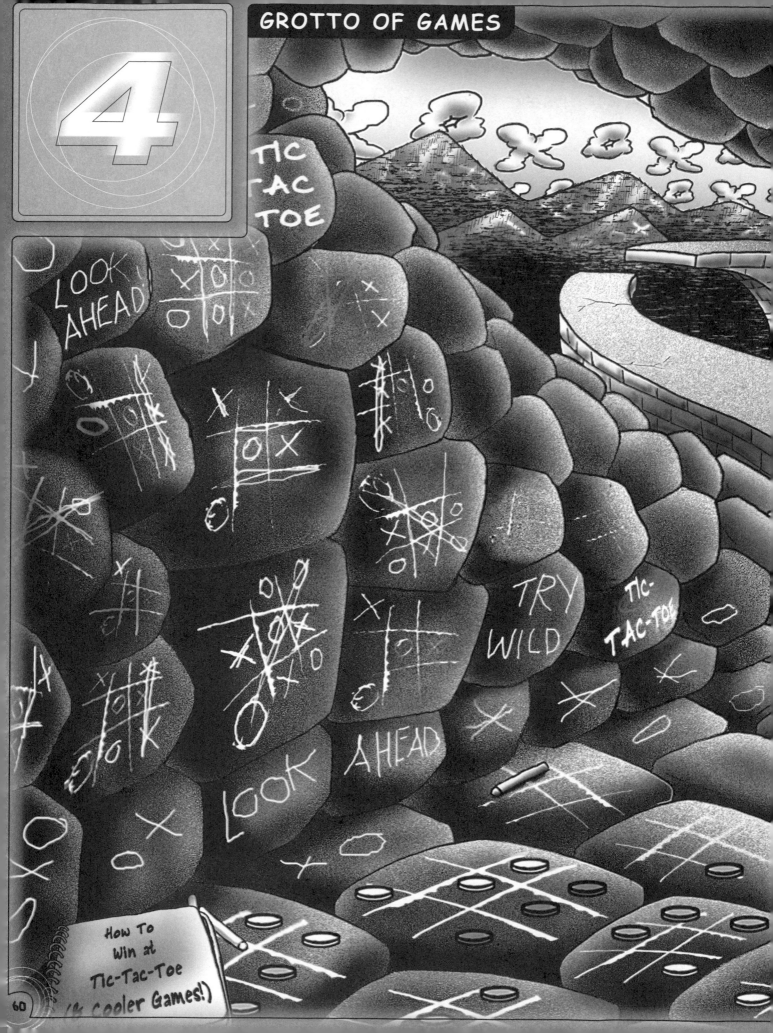

HOW TO WIN AT TIC-TAC-TOE
(and cooler games)

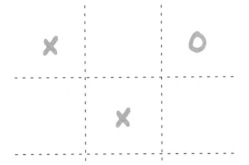

You probably already know how to play Tic-Tac-Toe. It's a really simple game, right? That's what most people think. But if you really wrap your brain around it, you'll discover that Tic-Tac-Toe isn't quite as simple as you think! That's what the Science-at-Home team discovered in the Grotto of Games.

Tic-Tac-Toe (along with a lot of other games) involves looking ahead and trying to figure out what the person playing against you might do next.

Scientists have found that playing games is one of the best ways to exercise your brain. The skills you use—looking at possibilities, seeing patterns, and making choices—are the same ones you use when you learn just about anything new.

In the next few pages, we'll show you 4 different games you can play with a Tic-Tac-Toe board.

WHAT DO I NEED?

For each game, you'll need:

- Someone to play the game with
- A pencil
- Some paper

For Dime-Tac-Toe you'll also need:

- 3 dimes
- 3 pennies

Every game is played on a grid that's 3 squares by 3 squares.

TIC-TAC-TOE

You may know how to play this simple game, but have you ever stopped to notice how and why you make your choices?

Try playing a few games. Then let's take a close look at what's happening.

RULES FOR TIC-TAC-TOE

1. The game is played on a grid that's 3 squares by 3 squares.

2. One player is **X**, the other is **O**. Players take turns putting their marks in empty squares.

3. The first player to get 3 of her marks in a row (up, down, across, or diagonally) is the winner.

4. When all 9 squares are full, the game is over. If no player has 3 marks in a row, the game ends in a tie.

HOW CAN I WIN AT TIC-TAC-TOE?

Strategy is figuring out what you need to do to win.

Let's say you're the **X**. Part of your strategy is trying to figure out how to get three **X**s in a row. The other part is trying to figure out how to stop the other player from getting three **O**s in a row.

LOOK AHEAD

After you put an **X** in a square, you start looking ahead. Where's the best place for your next **X**? You look at the empty squares, and decide which ones are good choices—which ones have the possibility of making 3 **X**s in a row.

KEEP AN EYE ON THE OTHER PLAYER

But you also have to watch where the other player puts her **O**. That could change what you do next. If she gets 2 **O**s in a row, you *have* to put your next **X** in the last empty square in that row, or she'll win. You're forced to play in a particular square or lose the game.

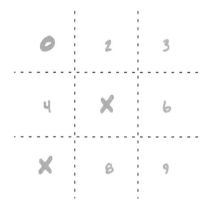

Here's a game that's just started.
X went first, then O, then X again.
Where's the best square for O to play next?
There are six empty squares, but O doesn't really have a choice, does she?
To stop X from getting 3 in a row,
O is forced to play in square #3.
That move blocks X.

What's X's next move?
There are two Os in the top row. So even though X has five squares to choose from, he's forced to play in square #2, because that will block O.
If both players continue to block each other, no one will get 3 in a row, and the game will end in a tie.

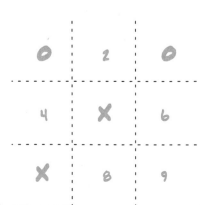

WHAT'S THE BEST FIRST MOVE?

There are 8 possible winning paths in Tic-Tac-Toe: 3 across, 3 up and down, and 2 diagonally. Where you put your first **X** will eliminate some of those paths for you.

The 9 empty squares at the start of the game can be grouped into three kinds—corner (4), border (4), or center (1). Each position has some advantages.

First Move to the Center

If you play to the center, you have 4 possible paths. Then O has 8 squares to choose from. O can play any of the other 4 paths— the top, bottom, and 2 sides. Any square that O chooses will block one of your paths. But on your next turn, no matter where O played, you'll have 3 of your 4 paths left.

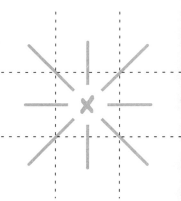

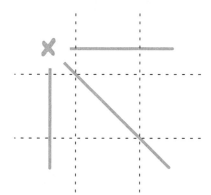

First Move to a Corner

If you play to one of the corners, you have 3 ways to win. Then O has 8 squares to choose from, and 5 possible paths to play. Only 6 of the empty squares will block you; 2 won't. Even if you're blocked, you will have 2 of your 3 paths left on your next turn.

First Move to a Border

If you play to one of the border squares, you have 2 ways to win. Only half of O's 8 choices will block you, but O has 6 possible paths to choose. If you are blocked, you'll have one of your 2 paths left on your next turn.

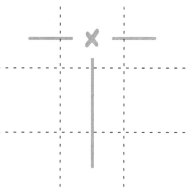

WHAT'S MY BEST MOVE IF I PLAY SECOND?

If **X** plays to the center, **O**'s best first move is to a corner, because then she has 2 possible winning paths, and leaves **X** with 3 paths. If she plays to a border, she still leaves **X** with 3 paths, but she only has one.

If **X** takes a border or a corner, **O**'s best first move is to take the center. Then she has 3 possible paths, and leaves **X** with one or 2 paths.

Experiment with some of the different opening moves and see where the **X**s and **O**s end up when the game's over.

If you always pay attention and look ahead, you'll never lose a game of Tic-Tac-Toe.

But you won't win much either. Most games will probably end in a tie.

On the next few pages are 3 other Tic-Tac-Toe games for you to experiment with. They're all played on the same 3 x 3 grid.

TOE-TAC-TIC

RULES FOR **TOE-TAC-TIC** Use exactly the same rules as regular Tic-Tac-Toe, except that the first person to get 3 in a row *loses*.

HOW CAN I WIN? Strategy in this game is about the same as the regular game. But until your brain gets used to the idea that 3 in a row is *bad*, you'll probably outsmart yourself the first few games.

When Dutch children win a game of Tic-Tac-Toe, they shout...

BOTER, MELK, EN KAAS! IK BEN DE BAAS!

IT MEANS "BUTTER, MILK, AND CHEESE! I AM THE BOSS!"

(IT SOUNDS BETTER IN DUTCH.)

WILD TIC-TAC-TOE

RULES FOR **WILD TIC-TAC-TOE**

The same as the regular game, except that both players can use either **X** or **O** on any turn.

HOW CAN I WIN? It's much harder to set up a win for yourself, because if you get two **X**s in a row, the other player can just play an **X** and win. This is a trickier game, and it's very easy to outsmart yourself.

Suppose the person who goes first plays to the center using an **X**. The second player *must* play an **O**.

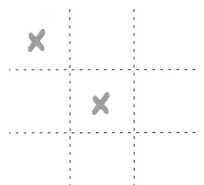

If the second player uses an X, no matter where he puts it, there will be two Xs in a row, and the first player will win on her next move.

Until both players get used to the different strategy, many games of Wild Tic-Tac-Toe will have a winner. After both players get the hang of it, the game will probably end in a tie. But it's a little more interesting than regular Tic-Tac-Toe, because you have more choices along the way.

DIME TIC-TAC-TOE

This is a really interesting version, full of traps and strategy. You'll need 3 dimes and 3 pennies to play it, using the same old 3 x 3 grid.

RULES FOR DIME TIC-TAC-TOE

1. One player (**A**) has the dimes, the other (**B**) has the pennies. **A** puts one coin in a square, then it's **B**'s turn.

2. The first player to get 3 coins in a row is the winner.

3. If all 6 coins are down, but there is no winner (no one has 3 in a row), then the game changes.

After **B** puts down his last penny, **A** gets to move one of her dimes, with these rules:

• A coin can only be moved one square at a time.
• A coin can only be moved into an empty square.
• No diagonal moves allowed; only right, left, up, or down.
• A coin can't jump over another coin.
• A player has to move when it's his or her turn.

4. **A** and **B** keep moving their coins, in turn, until someone gets 3 in a row and wins the game.

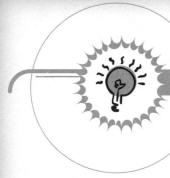

Until all six coins are played, Dime Tic-Tac-Toe is just like regular Tic-Tac-Toe. But once you start moving the coins around, it becomes a very different game. There are lots and lots of possible moves to choose from, and strategy becomes even more important. Here are some tips about moving the coins:

You can't move to just any empty square. You can only move a coin one square over. So watch out for getting yourself in a bind—having two coins in a row, but no way to move your third coin over to join them.

If you surround the other player's coins with yours, he can't move the trapped coin. (And your opponent can do the same to you.)

Sometimes you can trap the other player's coins so that her *only* choice is to move out of the square that you want to move into.

A SAMPLE GAME

The best way to find out how the game works is to play it, over and over. Here's a sample game to give you an idea of some of the possibilities.

The other player went first, playing dimes. You've got one penny left, and 4 squares to choose from. What's your best move?

Square #6

If you put your penny here, you can win in two more turns by moving the center penny to #8, then into #9. It'll take the dimes two moves to get 3 in a row, too, but he'll get there first. You'll lose. Not a good choice.

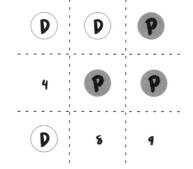

Square #8

This works about the same as #6. It'll take you two moves to win, and the dimes will beat you to the punch. Not a good choice.

Square #9

In regular Tic-Tac-Toe, this would be a goofy move. But look what will happen next. On your next turn, all you have to do is slide the penny in the center over into square #6. You win! And there's nothing the other player can do to block you. Excellent move.

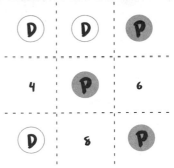

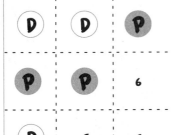

Square #4

This is also a great move. You'll win on your next turn, by sliding the penny in the corner down into square #6. And there's nothing the other player can do to stop you!

> When the Science-at-Home team was testing out Dime-Tac-Toe, some games went very fast—only a few moves. But some lasted as long as 10 minutes, with both players staring so intently at the board that someone asked if we were playing chess!

WHY BOTHER WITH TIC-TAC-TOE?

Tic-Tac-Toe is the same kind of game as chess, just a lot less complicated. Mathematicians who study game theory call those games "finite two-person contests with perfect information." What does all that mean? It means that the game always comes to a definite, recognizable end, and that you can know all the possible moves.

At the start of a game of Tic-Tac-Toe, there are lots of possible moves—362,880, to be exact. How can there be that many moves? The game starts with 9 empty squares, so the first person has 9 choices of where to put his mark. The second person has 8 empty squares left to choose from. Then **X** has 7 choices, **O** has 6, and so on until all the squares are full. The number 362,880 is 9 x 8 x 7 x 6 x 5 x 4 x 3 x 2 x 1. (A chess game has 10^{120} possible moves. That's a 1 followed by 120 zeroes!)

> TIC-TAC-TOE HAS 362,880 POSSIBLE MOVES

> A CHESS GAME HAS 10^{120} POSSIBLE MOVES.

Because Tic-Tac-Toe has a relatively small number of possible moves, it was one of the first games that scientists working on artificial intelligence (AI) programmed early computers to play. The goal of AI is to create machines that will "think" the way people do. That involves making decisions, using reason and logic, learning to recognize patterns, and analyzing possibilities. Which is exactly what you're doing when you play Tic-Tac-Toe.

WHAT NOW?

If you liked putting **X**s in boxes (and thinking logically about what might happen), go to the **Logic Lounge** on page 110.

If you liked playing games, visit **Leak Lake** on page 54 or "Hangman" in **Jumping the Gap** on page 52.

If you want to continue to explore the **Forest of Hidden Surprises**, turn the page.

5

Seeing
Double

SEEING DOUBLE

Take a look at the picture. What do you *see*? It looks like a fancy white vase, doesn't it? Or maybe a candlestick holder? But look again. Can you also see it as two people facing each other against a white background?

Sometimes, there are two completely different ways to look at the same thing. When a picture doesn't give you enough information to decide how to view it, your brain has to make a choice. The choice you make—vase or faces—may happen without you even realizing that you *are* making a choice. That's because a lot of the time, you don't realize that there are actually two ways to see the thing you're looking at.

You're going to look at pictures that you can see two different ways. At first, you'll probably see only one way to look at each picture. But keep looking and eventually you'll be able to train your brain to see the "other" picture. With practice, you may become an expert at "flipping" between the two pictures in your mind.

WHAT IS IT?

Guess what this picture is . . . then guess again.

WHAT DO I DO? Look at the picture. Do you see an animal? Look some more and see if you can see a different animal.

WHAT'S GOING ON? Depending on how you look at it, this could be a picture of a rabbit or of a duck. (The rabbit's ears become the duck's bill.)

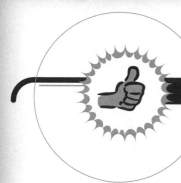

DOUBLE TROUBLE

Take a look at these two pictures.

Each can be seen as two completely different things. Try to find both. If you're stumped, go to page 133, where we give you hints that will help you see both pictures.

If you're having trouble seeing the second picture, try looking at the picture from a distance. Sometimes that helps.

WELCOME TO THE THIRD DIMENSION!

These illusions are designed to look three-dimensional. Instead of just sitting flat on the page, they seem to "pop out" at you. But depending on how you look at them, the pictures can pop out in two different ways.

WHAT DO I DO? **1.** Imagine this picture as a pup tent made of clear plastic. Which side looks like it's in front, and which side looks like it's in back?

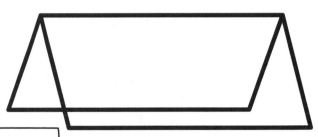

2. Can you mentally "flip" the picture, so that you see what used to be the front side as being in back?

3. If you're have trouble getting it to work, take a look at the pictures below. We've shaded one side of the pup tent so that you can see two different views. Look at the two views, then look back at the clear tent above. Can you "flip" the picture from one view to the other?

This is one way of looking at it . . .

. . . this is another way.

4. Now take a look at this picture. Imagine that it's a box made of clear plastic. Find the small star in the upper left corner of one of the cube's faces. Does the face with the star look like it's up front, or in the back? Can you get it to switch?

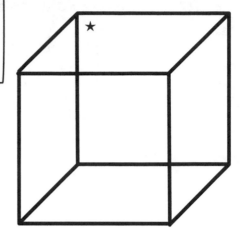

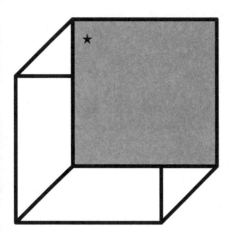

With the star up front, the box looks like this.

With the star in back, the box looks like this.

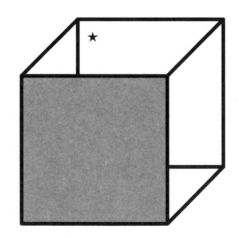

5. Practice flipping back and forth between the two views. How long does it take to switch each time? The more you do it, the easier it gets.

WHAT ELSE CAN I DO? Now try just staring at the cube. Notice which face is in front, but don't try to change it. Stare at it for a minute or so. Chances are, the cube will flip back and forth all by itself!

ONE MORE ILLUSION TO TRY

Which do you see: a long hallway or a pyramid with its top cut off?

Most people see the hallway easily but have a little trouble seeing the pyramid. This shaded view may make it easier to see. (The white square is the cut-off top of the pyramid.)

Once you can see it both ways, see how quickly you can switch between them.

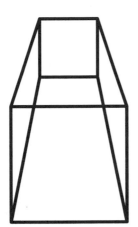
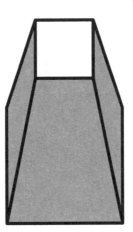

WHY DO THESE ILLUSIONS "FLIP"? When you gaze at the illusions in this chapter, you may find that what you see flips back and forth between the two possible views. First one face of the cube is up front, then the other one is. Now you see a duck, now you see a rabbit . . . without even trying! What gives?

Psychologists have two theories about why illusions like these flip back and forth. The first is that it depends which part of the figure you're looking at. Focusing on the bill makes you see a duck. Focusing on the rabbit's nose makes you see a rabbit.

The other theory is that your brain gets tired of looking at it one way, and switches to the other way to give itself a break. When you look at the duck/rabbit picture, the part of your brain that recognizes rabbits says "Hey! it's a rabbit! A rabbit! Yep, a rabbit. Still a rabbit . . ." Eventually, your brain gets so tired of looking at the rabbit, it says "Hey! It's a duck!" instead.

IMPOSSIBLE PICTURES

These illusions are called impossible because they show three-dimensional objects that couldn't exist in the real world.

WHAT DO I DO? Look carefully at each drawing and notice how your brain "flips" between two ways of seeing it.

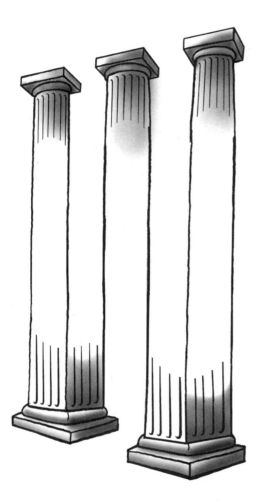

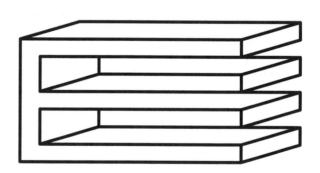

WHAT'S GOING ON? Each impossible picture is actually made up of two different half-pictures that have been cleverly blended together. On its own, each half-picture makes sense. But if you put them together, the two halves don't agree. Your brain flips back and forth between them, believing whichever one it's focused on at the time.

A VERY SHORT STORY

Read the sentence below.

THE CAT ATE THE RAT

WHAT'S GOING ON? If you take a closer look at the "A"s and "H"s in this phrase, you'll notice they're exactly the same shape. Still, you were probably able to read the phrase with no trouble.

When you see something that can be interpreted two different ways, your brain chooses to see the thing that seems to make the most sense. To read this sentence, your brain made 5 quick choices about whether to see an H or an A, probably before you even noticed that something was unusual. That's quick thinking!

SO WHAT?

Have you ever tried to read a note from someone with really bad handwriting? A lot of the words are almost impossible to read. But you can figure out what they say by looking at the surrounding words and guessing what would make sense.

Whether you're reading words or looking at pictures, sometimes it's impossible to know what you're looking at without looking at the stuff around it. The surroundings can give you clues that tell you what's likely to be true. Another word for surrounding stuff that tells you what something means is context.

When things are removed from their usual surroundings, they can be much harder to identify. If you bumped into someone from your swimming class at the library, it might take you a second to remember him. That's because you're used to seeing him in a different context.

WHAT NOW?

If you like seeing shapes in a new way, go to **A Shift at the Snack Bar** on page 102 or **Temple of Tan** on page 82.

If you liked catching a glimpse of something unexpected, visit **Moonstruck on the Mountain** on page 42.

If you like stuff that tricks your mind, try out some tricky memories at the **Lost and Found** on page 18 or **Treasure Chest** on page 34.

If you want to continue to explore the **Forest of Hidden Surprises**, turn the page to find more illusions.

6

Don't Believe
Everything
You See

DON'T BELIEVE EVERYTHING YOU SEE

Which statue on the page at left is bigger? Well, the one in the back *looks* bigger. But you'd better get out your ruler and measure them to be sure. You can't always trust your eyes, here in the Garden of Illusions.

Take a look at the two horizontal lines below. Which one looks longer?

Most people think the one on the left looks a little longer. Actually, the two lines are the same length.

The arrows and the statues are *optical illusions*, pictures that fool you into seeing something that's not true. Most optical illusions (including these) work by fooling your brain.

You can experiment with optical illusions, learn how they work, and make some of your own.

TRICKY TABLES

These two tables look completely different—but are they?

WHAT DO I NEED?
- A pencil
- A piece of tracing paper or typing paper

WHAT DO I DO?

1. Look at the two tables. Do they look like they're the same size or shape?

2. Lay a piece of paper on top of one of the tables. Trace the outline of the tabletop. Now take the tracing you made and try lining it up with the *other* tabletop. Believe it or not, they're exactly the same size!

Which of the two horizontal lines looks longer?

Most people think the horizontal line on top looks longer. But they're the same size. If you don't believe it, you can check by measuring them with a ruler.

WHAT'S GOING ON? One of the ways that we figure out the size of things in the world around us is by guessing how far away they are. We know that when things are far away, they look smaller. So we automatically assume that faraway things are bigger than they look.

It's hard to believe the two tables on page 77 are the same size and shape. The table on the left looks so long partly because one end of it seems to be farther away. The back end seems to stretch off into the distance, making the table look longer than it really is.

These slanting lines also create an illusion of distance. Have you ever stood in the middle of a long, straight road? The sides of the road look like they get closer and closer together as they get farther away from you, sort of like the two lines in this picture. When you look at this picture, your brain decides that the slanting lines are like the sides of the road and the horizontal line on top is farther away. Since it's farther away, your brain figures it must be bigger than it looks.

We also judge size by making comparisons. If two things are side by side, and we know how big one of them is, we can use it to estimate the size of the other thing. What happens when you compare the horizontal lines to the slanting lines of the road? The bottom line looks less than half as wide as the road, while the top line seems to reach almost all the way across the road. So again, the top line looks bigger.

TOTALLY WARPED

Drawing a straight line is harder than you think!

WHAT DO I NEED? • A photocopy of this page
• A pencil
• A ruler

WHAT DO I DO? **1.** Using your ruler, draw a line connecting point A to point B, and another line connecting point C to point D.

2. Now take a look at the lines you've drawn. Chances are, the lines in Box 1 seem to bulge away from each other, and the lines in Box 2 seem to bulge towards each other.

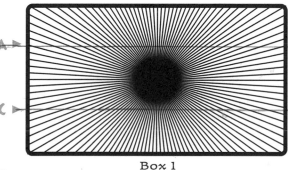

Box 1

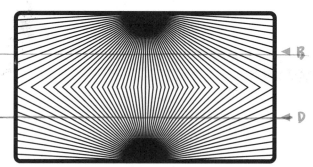

Box 2

WHAT'S GOING ON? Our brains have a funny problem with judging angles. No one really knows why, but when you look at angles that are sharp, your brain tends to see them as slightly wider than they really are. Angles that are wide look slightly less wide than they really are.

Your brain sees this angle as if it was slightly less pointy than it really is.

Your brain sees this angle as if it was slightly more pointy than it really is.

Each of the lines you drew to make these illusions crossed the lines of the background at a different angle. Since your brain sees each of these angles differently, the lines you drew ended up looking bent.

CRAZY TILES

Are these tiles crooked?

This is one of the most amazing illusions we've ever seen. The tiles look crooked, don't they? They're not. Each tile is perfectly square, and the horizontal lines between the tiles are perfectly parallel.

If you're having trouble believing that the tiles aren't crooked, try looking at one or two tiles at a time, blocking out the rest of the tiles with your hand. Or use a piece of paper to block out all but the top or bottom row of tiles. Do they still look crooked?

Here's another way to convince yourself the lines aren't crooked. Close one eye, hold this page up just under your nose, and look across the page along the horizontal lines.

Why does it work?
No one is really sure.

ILLUSIONS IN THE REAL WORLD

Optical illusions like these are lurking all around you, in places you'd least suspect. One of the most well-known "real-world" illusions is called the moon illusion.

WHAT DO I DO? Have you ever noticed that the full moon looks really big when it's near the horizon, and smaller when it's high in the sky?

Next time you see the full moon on the horizon, hold your hand out at arm's length and cover the moon with a finger. Can you block it with a single finger, maybe just the tip of your pinky?

Later in the night, when the moon is high in the sky, try the same thing again. The moon will look smaller high in the sky, but if you measure it against your outstretched hand, you'll see that it's the same size as before.

No one's exactly sure why the moon illusion happens. One idea is that the moon looks smaller overhead because there's nothing to compare it to. Another possibility is that your brain exaggerates the size of things near the horizon, thinking they're farther away than things overhead.

SO WHAT?

Sometimes, there's a big difference between what you see and what's really there.

Take an ordinary drinking glass. If you hold it right next to your eye, it looks enormous. If it's across the room, it looks tiny. If you look at it from above, it looks like a circle. If you look at it from the side, it's a completely different shape.

To make sense of this confusing world, your brain looks for clues that help you figure out what's going on. You remember things you've seen before and make use of that past experience to figure out what's going on here. Many optical illusions rely on what your brain *expects* to see in the world and use that expectation to fool you.

Optical illusions are more than just silly puzzles for your eyes and brain. Scientists who are interested in how you see the world experiment with optical illusions. By fooling your eyes and brain, they can figure out some of the shortcuts that your brain takes in making sense of the world.

WHAT NOW?

If you want to be fooled some more, go to **Through the Trapdoor** on page 98.

If you want to see other ways your brain can be fooled, go to **Treasure Chest** on page 34.

If you want to try a different optical illusion, visit "The Triangle That Isn't There" in **Jumping the Gap** on page 51.

If you want to try some puzzles that make the visual part of your brain work hard, check out **A Shift at the Snack Bar** on page 102.

If you want to continue to explore the **Forest of Hidden Surprises,** turn the page.

Puzzling Patterns

PUZZLING PATTERNS

You're on the path to the Puzzle House now, but you're not quite done with the Forest of Hidden Surprises. Here at the Temple of Tan, we found some puzzles that contain hidden surprises. To make pictures like the ones on the Temple, you combine simple shapes in surprising ways.

The geometric shapes that make up the Temple fit together to make pictures in a fascinating game called *tangrams.*

MAKING YOUR TANGRAM SET

Before you can play with tangrams, you need to make a set of tans, the simple shapes that you use to make pictures.

WHAT DO I NEED?
• A pair of scissors
• A photocopy of this page or a piece of typing paper and a pencil

WHAT DO I DO? **1.** If you have a photocopy of this page, cut out the square. Then cut along the black lines to divide the square into 7 pieces.

2. If you don't have a photocopy, put your typing paper on top of the square. Trace the square and the black lines. Then cut along the black lines to divide the square into 7 pieces.

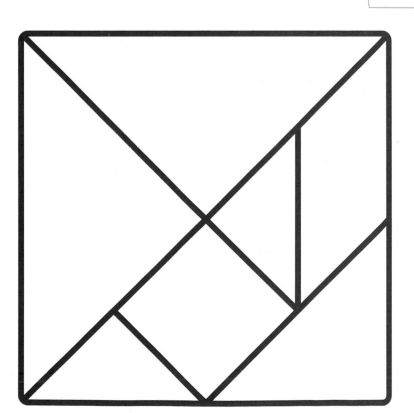

Now you have a square, 2 small triangles, 2 large triangles, a medium-sized triangle, and a parallelogram. These pieces are called tans. You can use your tans to do all the puzzles in this chapter.

GETTING WARMED UP

Usually, people play tangrams by making figures that use all 7 tans. But before you do that, you might want to try these warm-up exercises. They'll help you get familiar with the tans and how they fit together, which will help you solve the puzzles.

TRICKY TRIANGLE Use some of the tans to make a triangle that's exactly the same size and shape as one of the big tangram triangles. The tans must fit together and they can't overlap.

How many different ways can you do this? We came up with 2.

PERPLEXING POLYGON Can you use some of the tans to make a shape that looks like this? We found 3 different ways to do it.

See page 133 for our solutions.

MAKE AN EAGLE

Now that you're warmed up, here's how people have been playing with tangrams for hundreds of years. Try making this picture of an eagle using all 7 of your tans. All the tans must touch, but they can't overlap.

When you try this, you may discover that making this figure using all 7 tans is harder than it looks. If you get stuck, read the "Helpful Hints" on the next page.

Yes, you really do have to use all 7 tans.

See page 133 for our solutions.

HELPFUL HINTS

LOOK FOR SHAPES IN THE FIGURE THAT LOOK LIKE ONE PARTICULAR TAN

In the eagle, it looks like the wings must be the 2 big triangles. So you might want to put those pieces in place first. And it looks like the eagle is standing on the middle-sized triangle. So put that triangle at the bottom. It looks like the shape right above that triangular base might be the square, so put that in place, too.

TAKE YOUR TIME—AND TAKE A SECOND LOOK

You have just 3 pieces left—2 small triangles and a parallelogram. Look very carefully at the head and the neck of the eagle. How can you fit these pieces together so that you'll get a slanting line on the left side and a line that goes straight up on the right? Basically, you're trying to use these 3 pieces to make a shape that looks like this.

Take one of the tans and rotate it. As you do that, watch carefully to see how it could fit into this shape. Can you find a position that gives you the slanting line on the left side of the eagle's neck? If you can, you're almost there.

FOOL AROUND

Don't assume that your first guess is the right one. There are lots of ways to make the same shapes. Keep moving the tans around and trying different positions until you find one that fits.

The solution to this puzzle is on page 133.

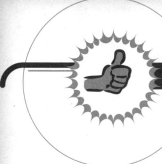
Use all 7 of your tans with no overlapping to make these pictures. If you get stuck, check out the Tangram Tips below and on the next page.

Running Lion

V is for Victory

The solutions are
on page 133.

The solutions are
on page 133.

TANGRAM TIPS

PUT THE DIFFICULT PIECES IN PLACE FIRST

The biggest tans are the toughest ones to place. In any figure, there are only a few places that they can fit. So put those pieces in place first—and go on from there. (If you're making the "V is for Victory" tangram, see if you can figure out where you can put the two big triangles first.)

EXPERIMENT

A tan can look very different when you rotate it. Different tans can fit together in many different ways. Here are 3 different combinations using a small triangle and a parallelogram.

DON'T ASSUME YOUR FIRST GUESS IS RIGHT

Sometimes, a square is a square—and sometimes it's 2 triangles, put together to make a square. If you get really stuck, see if there's another way to make one of the shapes in the design.

BE PATIENT

The more you play with tangrams, the better you'll get at solving these puzzles. Just when you think you've figured it all out, you'll see a new way to fit the tans together and get a new shape.

 ## TANGRAMANIA!

If you liked those tangram puzzles, here are some more to try.

If you want to turn this into a game, make another set of tans for a friend and see who can make a particular design first!

The solutions are on page 133.

MAKE YOUR OWN TANGRAM PUZZLES

Invent your own tangram puzzles and challenge other people to solve them!

WHAT DO I DO? **1.** Make your own puzzle by putting the 7 tans together to make a picture.

2. Copy the picture, but don't show the lines between the different tans.

3. Give friends your drawing and the tans, and challenge them to solve your puzzle.

Here's a puzzle that Pat Murphy of the Science-at-Home team made. She says that it's an alien, just out of a flying saucer.

(You can try to make Pat's alien. The solution is on page 133.)

HOW CAN I STUMP MY FRIENDS? It's easy to figure out tangram designs where the pieces only meet at the corners like this:

If you want to make a puzzle that's challenging for someone else to solve, be sure to push the tans together so that some tans meet all along their sides, like this:

BE SQUARE

You made all 7 tans from one square of paper, right? Can you put them back together into a square again?

The solution is on page 133.

WHAT'S GOING ON?

These puzzles may be hard at first, but you'll get better at them if you keep playing with the tans. At first, you can only see a few ways to put the tans together. Just keep pushing them around, rotating them, and trying different combinations. You'll find possibilities that you didn't see at first.

When you're trying to solve a puzzle, it may seem like you have one piece too few or one piece too many. Then you see a way to change what you've got. You may have thought you had to use the medium-sized triangle to make part of the figure, but then you realize that you can make the shape you need from two different pieces. Suddenly—surprise!—everything falls into place. When that happens, you get an enormous sense of satisfaction.

We don't know why it feels so great to solve a puzzle. Maybe it has something to do with the human need to find order in the world. Maybe it has to do with the pleasure you get when you see something new, something you've never seen before. Whatever the reason, we know that great feeling of satisfaction is what brings us back to tangrams and other puzzles again and again.

WHAT NOW?

If you like tricky puzzles that involve shapes, check out **A Shift at the Snack Bar** on page 102.

If you want to try fitting letters together, rather than shapes, visit **Leak Lake** on page 54.

If you liked seeing how things fit together in unexpected ways, go to the **Playroom** on page 124.

If you liked challenging a friend to solve your tangram puzzle, challenge your friend to a game in the **Grotto of Games** on page 60.

If you'd like to continue on to the **Puzzle House,** turn the page.

PUZZLE HOUSE

The path from the Forest of Hidden Surprises led you to a treehouse—the Puzzle House. As you explore, question everything and try anything. To try the puzzles in a room, turn to the page numbers shown.

CAN YOU FIGURE OUT WHAT THESE STRANGE NOTES MEAN?

PLEXER STUDIO **PAGE 92**

Never Assume Anything

Where do the largest carrots grow?

FOR MORE TRICKY QUESTIONS AND THEIR ANSWERS, SEE PAGE 99.

THROUGH THE TRAPDOOR **PAGE 98**

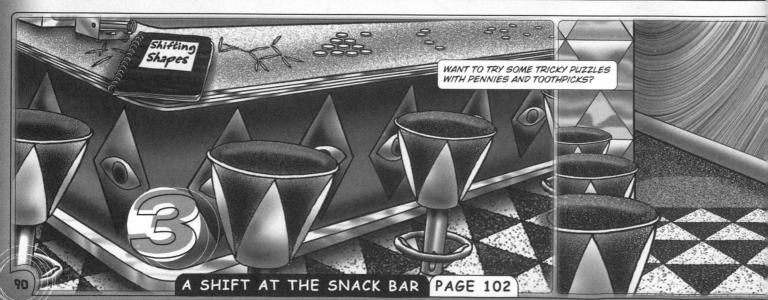

Shifting Shapes

WANT TO TRY SOME TRICKY PUZZLES WITH PENNIES AND TOOTHPICKS?

A SHIFT AT THE SNACK BAR **PAGE 102**

Detectives Needed!
Within this room are many mysteries to be unraveled.
If your powers of observation are keen, and you're good at putting clues together, you may enter.
Logical thinking is the only tool you need.
whatever remains must be the truth"
-Sherlock Holmes
Unsolved Cases
PUZZLE POLICE LINE - DO NOT CROSS
4
PU
SH
MYSTERIES IN THE LOGIC LOUNGE PAGE 110

BEND YOUR BRAIN AROUND THESE BAFFLING BEGINNINGS!
PU
5
A
9
B
2
Beginnings
BOOK OF BEGINNINGS PAGE 120

CREATIVE PEOPLE ARE WILLING TO MAKE A MESS.

From the top of the Puzzle House, the world is laid out at your feet. You can see the Forest of Hidden Surprises and the mouth of the cave that leads to the Caverns of Memory. Where would you like to go now?

6
PLAYROOM PAGE 124

PLEXERS

Look at the words below. They describe the way someone might order breakfast in a restaurant.

EGGS

EASY

The trick to solving the puzzle isn't just reading the words, it's noticing how they're arranged. The word "eggs" is on top of the word "easy," so the solution to the puzzle is: Eggs over easy.

In some puzzle books, puzzles like these are called *plexers*, because they're perplexing. They're designed to *mean* something more than what they actually say. Other books call them *rebuses* (or *rebi*). Usually a rebus is a drawing of something that sounds like a letter or a word—like a picture of a bee for the letter B. In this case, the word itself is the picture

 **SOME PERPLEXING PLEXERS**

Try to figure out these plexers.

1.

**ARREST
YOU'RE**

2.

SOMEWHERE
———————————
RAINBOW

3.

**ONCE
TIME**

4.

K CLOCK O

(R above, C below)

5.

TULIPS

(T, I, P above; T, O, E below)

6.

GNIKOOL

On page 94 you'll find some tips on how to break open a plexer that has you baffled. The solutions are on page 134.

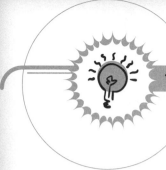

TIPS FOR SOLVING PLEXERS

CHECK YOUR PREPOSITIONS

A preposition is a word that tells you where (or sometimes when) something is done. A lot of plexers depend on prepositions like "above," "below," "on," "under," "after," and so on.

The first thing you should do when you see a plexer is to look carefully at the positions of the words. If they're stacked on top of each other, the solution may have something to do with "over" or "under." But don't jump to conclusions.

Take a look at "eggs over easy" on page 93. You could read it as "easy under eggs" or "eggs on easy" or "eggs above easy" or "easy below eggs"—and you wouldn't be any closer to solving the puzzle.

PULL THE PLEXER APART

What if you have a plexer that looks like it's all one word—but it's a word that makes no sense? Try looking for little words inside the big one—then notice the position of the words. Here's an example:

J O A N B

It looks like a girl's name and the letter B. What other word can you find in that arrangement of letters? OA isn't a word. Neither is NB. But AN is. What word do you have if you take the letters AN away? You're left with JOB. And so you might figure out that the solution to this particular plexer is

AN inside JOB—an inside job

Groan. A lot of plexers turn out to be bad puns once you figure them out. (See page 97 to find out more about puns.)

WHAT DO YOU SEE?

When you're trying to figure out a plexer, it sometimes helps to talk out loud about what you're seeing. In a lot of plexers, the word on the page is part of the solution, so hearing it out loud may give your brain a clue or a connection. In other plexers, the shape of the word is important. What does it look like? Is it bent? Turned over? Backward? Really big? Describing exactly what you're seeing may give you the clue that will lead you to the solution.

MORE PLEXERS

Some of these may be easy for you to figure out, but others may fry your brain.

If you get stuck, the solutions are on page 134.

7.
PINEAPPLE ƆꓘA⅃Ɔ

8.
ME ME ME
AL AL AL

9.
RRRRRRR
RRRRRRR
RRRRRRR
RRRRRRR
RRRRRRR
RRRRRRR
RRRRRRR

10.
SOME I'M THING

11.
P P

12.
PROMISE

13.
R A D
  A
R O I L

14.
STORM
any port

MAKING YOUR OWN PLEXERS

Create some new puzzles of your own.

THE CAT IN THE HAT

READING BETWEEN THE LINES

BEATING AROUND THE BUSH

THE INSIDE STORY

A HOLE IN ONE

ALICE IN WONDERLAND

SHRINKING VIOLET

HOW DO I START?

To make a plexer, you need to start with a common phrase that most people will know or recognize. If you use a phrase that only you know, no one else will be able to solve your plexer.

Where can you find plexer-ready phrases? Maybe in a slogan you hear on TV. Or in an old saying. Or in the title of a favorite book. Here are a few ideas to get you started.

SKATING ON THIN ICE

MAN OVERBOARD

GROWING PAINS

I'VE GOT A PHRASE. NOW WHAT?

Look at the parts of the phrase. Let's play with READING BETWEEN THE LINES. It's got 3 parts: reading, between, and lines. Think about how you could show or draw each part.

There's not much to do with READING except write it down as a word. But you *can* fiddle with the idea of what it means to be "between," and with how you make lines.

Here are three different plexers made from that same phrase.

a.

LINE READING LINE

b.

| R | E | A | D | I | N | G |

c.

READING
‾‾‾‾‾‾‾

PLAY WITH SHAPES

Another way to make a plexer out of a phrase is to see whether you can use any of the words as pictures or shapes. Here are 3 different plexers made from another phrase: A HOLE IN ONE.

a. **1** H

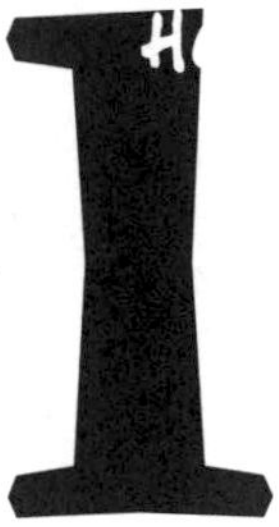

b. **1**

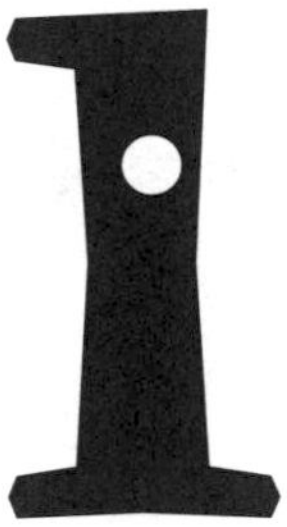

c. **O**HOLE **NE**

ADD A COLORFUL TOUCH

When you're making your own plexers, you can do something that we couldn't do in this book. You can play around with color. Here are 3 words that will become plexers when you color each of them with the right crayon. Can you figure out which colors to use?

Can you think of other plexers that will only work in color?

ENCYCLOPEDIA

THUMB

MOON (ONCE)

The solutions are on page 134.

PLAY AROUND WITH OTHER PLEXERS Try messing around with some of the plexers in the Plexer Studio. Maybe you can come up with a new way to show the same thing. That's one of the qualities of creative people—they don't limit themselves to just one solution to a problem. While you're thinking about how to show the idea of "over" or "between," your brain will probably start remembering other phrases with those words, too.

KEEP YOUR EYES—AND EARS—OPEN Once you get your brain into puzzle gear, it's hard *not* to find plexer material almost everywhere—while you're reading, watching TV, or listening to other people talk. Even simple phrases that you've heard 100 times, like "He's in big trouble," may begin to turn themselves into plexers, like the one below:

KEEP TRACK OF POSSIBLE PLEXERS Make a list of all the prepositions you can think of, or phrases that you hear that stick in your brain. Then even after you've left the Plexer Studio, you'll have a ready-made plexer kit to fool around with.

TROU HE'S BLE

THE ART OF THE PUN

A pun is a play on words. Puns use a word that has more than one meaning, or a word that sounds like another word. Most riddles and a lot of jokes (and plexers) are based on puns.

I sat on the beach and watched the sun rise.
Big deal. I sat on a chair and watched the kitchen sink.
(The word "sink" has 2 different meanings.)

Why is a man with a cold like a pony?
He's a little hoarse.
(The words "horse" and "hoarse" don't mean the same thing at all, but they sound alike when you say them out loud.)

> WHY IS A MAN WITH A COLD LIKE A PONY?

> HE'S A LITTLE HOARSE.

Puns are one of the oldest kinds of humor—and many people say they're also the lowest kind. Puns are the kinds of jokes that usually make people groan when you tell them. But every time you hear a pun and groan, there are a lot of complex processes going on in your brain. In order to "get" a pun, you have to understand both meanings, which means that you're thinking on more than one level at the same time. Scientists believe that's a very important skill when you're being creative or trying to solve a problem.

A lot of plexers are visual puns. If you're stumped by a plexer, think about ways that a word or a shape or an arrangement of letters might have another meaning. Try reading the words out loud. With some plexers, there is a pun because the word on the page sounds like another word, and that word means something completely different.

WHAT NOW?

If you like seeing the unexpected, visit **Jumping the Gap** on page 48.

If you want to try another kind of word puzzle, go to the **Book of Beginnings** on page 120 or **Leak Lake** on page 54.

If you like other puzzles with puns in them, go to **Through the Trapdoor** on page 98, or **Cave Paintings** on page 30.

If you want to continue to explore the **Puzzle House,** turn the page.

NEVER ASSUME ANYTHING

Can you connect the 4 dots using 3 straight lines? You can only go through each dot once, and you can't lift your pencil once you've started. Stop and try it before you read any farther.

• •

• •

Not too hard, huh? If you draw a Z-shape (or an N, or a U), you can connect all 4 dots—zip, zip, zip. So let's make it a little trickier.

This time, your lines have to return to where they started. Your third line must end right back at the beginning of your first line. Give that a try. It really is possible.

Here's a hint.
Think of a shape that's made up of 3 straight lines.
Don't keep reading until you've given it your best shot.

If you're stumped, the solution is on page 134.

GOING OUTSIDE THE BOX

If you're like most people, you probably thought your lines had to stay inside the square box made by the dots. You assumed that was part of the rules. But it wasn't. If you thought it was, you probably got stuck. To solve the puzzle, you have to go outside the box.

Making an assumption means you decided something too soon. You made up your mind before you looked at all the possibilities. You decided there was a rule you had to follow, or that something *had* to be true.

In problem solving, any assumption may be a trap. And you can fall into your own trap and get stuck. Then the puzzle seems impossible. To get unstuck, question everything. Don't take anything for granted. You can practice with the puzzles on the next few pages.

ONE WORD ANSWER

Rearrange the letters below to make one word.

NEWDOOR

The solution is on page 134.

TRICKY TOOTHPICKS

To try this, you'll need 12 toothpicks. Use them to make this figure.

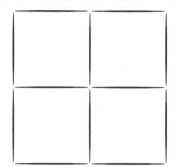

Now, move only 2 toothpicks, and make a figure with 7 squares.

The solution is on page 134.

HEY, THAT'S A TRICK! Yep. Most puzzles are written to be tricky. They're written so that you'll make assumptions, limit your choices, and get stuck in your own traps. So read everything very carefully.

If you do get stuck, it sometimes helps to show the puzzle to someone else and talk about how you're trying to solve it. The other person may be able to help you see the trap you've fallen into.

If you're really stuck and frustrated and feel like you're just beating your head against the same wall, over and over—stop. Look at the solution. No one can solve every puzzle, and once you know what the trick (or trap) was, you probably won't be fooled by it again.

TRAPPED IN THE TERRIBLE JOKE PIT

Each of these jokes has a trap. So remember—don't assume that anything has to be true. After you've figured out the traps (or fallen into them), you can spring them on your friends!

1. What's the best side of a teacup to put the handle on?

2. Where do the longest carrots grow?

3. What's unusual about the number 8549176320?

4. Which would you rather have, an old ten-dollar bill or a new one?

5. A butcher is 43 years old and stands 6'2" tall. What does he weigh?

6. When does this grouping of numbers make sense? 10, 2, 7 = 650

7. Six kids built a treehouse in two days. How long will it take 3 kids to build the same treehouse?

The solutions are on page 134.

THE BRAIN-BUSTER STORIES

Each of these stories may seem impossible at first. That's a good place to start to figure out the solution. Why do you think it's impossible? What are you assuming? What else could be going on?

Some stories may take a little while to unravel, but the more you can avoid making up your mind about what must be happening, the easier it'll be to avoid the traps.

The solutions are on page 134.

ALL IN THE FAMILY A man and his son were on a tour of an atomic power plant. In the control room, the boy asked if he could see the controls for the reactor core. The head physicist said yes, and explained how the controls worked. After the boy left, the head physicist turned to an assistant and said, "That was my son." How could that be?

THE RIVER ROVERS Three kids from Madison, Wisconsin, went for a hike. About a mile into the hike, they came to a deep, wide creek. There was no bridge. They didn't have a boat or a raft, or any materials to make one. None of them could swim. How did they get across?

THE STRANGE RACE Bill and Jason decided to have a reverse bike race. They'd start at the school playground and ride 15 miles into the country, have a picnic, then ride back. The catch was that the last bike to get back to the playground would be the winner.

They started at 10 in the morning, and rode fast and furiously, getting to the picnic spot just before noon. After they ate their sandwiches, Jason fell asleep. Bill immediately rode back to the playground as fast as he could. Why?

THE MATH TEST Everyone at Table Six was working hard on the math test. Jenny wrote down the last equation: 9 + 9 = 18. Then she put down her pencil. Susan was sitting across the table, and when Jenny wasn't looking, Susan copied her last answer.

Even though Susan copied the answer exactly, she got it wrong and Jenny got it right. How come? (No one discovered that Susan had been cheating.)

THE JUMPING HORSE This is a true story. A white horse jumped over a tower and landed on a priest, who immediately disappeared from the landscape. Where did this take place?

IT'S IN THE BAG One night, Chris left his home. He was wearing a mask and carrying an empty sack. He very methodically walked around the neighborhood, noting which houses were dark. An hour later, after taking at least one thing from 15 different houses, he returned home to examine the loot. Chris was not a burglar. What was going on?

BARNYARD BAFFLER Lisa walked out the back door of the farmhouse on a Thursday afternoon and was surprised to discover a man's pipe, a scarf, and three charcoal briquettes lying on the wet grass near the barn. The nearest neighbors lived a mile away, and no one had visited that day. Where did the objects come from?

WHAT NOW?

If you like riddles and puns, check out the **Plexer Studio** on page 92 or **Cave Paintings** on page 30.

If you want to experiment with traps that your memory sets for you, visit **Treasure Chest** on page 34.

If you like the feeling you get when you see something in a new way, go to **Trickery Thicket** on page 68.

If you want to try to escape some other brain traps, check out **Jumping the Gap** on page 48 or turn the page and go to **A Shift at the Snack Bar.**

If you want to continue to explore the **Puzzle House,** turn the page.

SHIFTING SHAPES

These puzzles look simple—and that's one of the things that makes them so tricky. All you have to do is shift a few coins or move a few toothpicks to find the solution. The question is: Which ones do you move?

Why bother to bend your mind around these puzzles? Well, it gives you a chance to wake your mind up to lots of creative possibilities. And it feels really good when you finally figure out the solution. It's also fun to use one of these puzzles to stump a friend, a teacher, or even your parents.

WHAT DO I NEED? To do all the puzzles in the Snack Bar, you need:
• 16 toothpicks (or wooden matches, or birthday candles)
• 10 pennies
• Tracing paper or typing paper
• A colored pencil or marker

PENNY TRIANGLE

WHAT DO I DO? Make this triangle out of 10 pennies.

Here's your challenge. Moving only 3 pennies, can you make a triangle that points down instead of up? The new triangle should look just like the one above, only flipped upside down.

See page 104 for a hint.

NEED A HINT? You know what the new triangle should look like, you just don't know how to get there. So one thing you could do is compare the "start" with the "finish" and see what's different.

You can do this by making a sketch of the triangle you're trying to make, one that points down. Just put a piece of tracing paper or typing paper over the picture of the pennies, trace the circles with a colored pencil, then flip the new picture over so it points down.

Look at your tracing and the picture on page 103. Do you see the 3 pennies that the 2 drawings *don't* have in common?

If you can't see them, try laying your tracing on top of the penny picture. Slide the tracing around until the two pictures match up as much as possible. Can you find the 3 pennies in each drawing that don't line up with anything in the other drawing? These are the ones you'll need to move.

See page 135 for the solution.

FISH FLIP

WHAT DO I **DO?** Make this goldfish out of 8 toothpicks.

Can you make the goldfish swim in the opposite direction by moving only 3 toothpicks?

NEED A HINT? Leaving the body where it is and switching the fins would require 4 moves. You only have 3. So you *can't* leave the body where it is. How can you make a new body out of some of the fins?

If you're still stuck, try the tracing paper method. You know that the new fish should look just like the old fish, just flipped in the other direction. Make a tracing of the fish above, then flip it over so it faces left instead of right. Lay the tracing on top of the picture and see if you can line the 2 pictures up so that only 3 toothpicks are different.

The solution is on page 135.

GET YOUR GOAT

WHAT DO I DO? Make this "goat" out of 5 toothpicks.

Can you move just **ONE** toothpick to make a goat that faces a different direction? The new goat should be exactly the same shape as the old one.

NEED A HINT? Even though you only need to move one toothpick, this puzzle is surprisingly hard. When we were trying to figure this one out, most of us on the Science-at-Home expedition got stuck. Here are some things that helped us get unstuck.

Vivian found it helpful to walk around the table and look at the puzzle from lots of different angles.

Ellen decided to try to rule out possible moves. She pointed out that the head and neck are the most complicated part of the puzzle, and that they can't really move because they go together, and that would mean moving 2 toothpicks. That leaves the 3 toothpicks that make up the body of the goat as the only possibilities.

Pat decided to use the tracing paper method. She traced the goat above and lined the 2 goats up so only one toothpick was different.

DON'T READ THE NEXT TWO PARAGRAPHS UNTIL YOU'VE TRIED THE PUZZLE!
The solution is on page 135.

NEED A HINT? Most people have trouble with this puzzle because of assumptions they don't even know they have. For example, you might have been thinking that each toothpick could only be the same body part as it started out being: A leg has to stay a leg. This may be true with real goats, but there is no such rule here. A toothpick is just a toothpick.

You may also have slowed yourself down by assuming that the new goat would be standing "on the ground"—that is, with both legs pointing down. There is no "ground" in the picture, but you may have created an imaginary ground in your mind. (Goats have to stand on something, don't they?) Walking around the table and looking at the puzzle from different angles helps shake that imaginary ground out of your head.

WHAT DO I **DO?** Make the shape to the right out of 15 toothpicks.

Can you remove 3 toothpicks and leave only 3 squares?
Every toothpick that remains has to be part of a square.

NEED A HINT? This is a different kind of toothpick puzzle. In this puzzle, you *don't* know what the final shape should look like. That's for you to figure out. So tracing the shape won't help you here as it did in the other puzzles. What *can* help you?

Let's take a close look at the problem. You're supposed to take 3 toothpicks away from the 15 you started with and end up with 3 squares. You could just try taking away toothpicks randomly, but there's a little math trick that will help rule out some possibilities. Here's how it works.

How many toothpicks does it take to make two separate squares, like this?

How many toothpicks does it take to make two attached squares, like this?

The separate squares need 8 toothpicks—4 toothpicks each—but the attached squares only need 7 because they share one "wall." You can use this fact to help you solve the puzzle.

Go to the top of the next page to find out how.

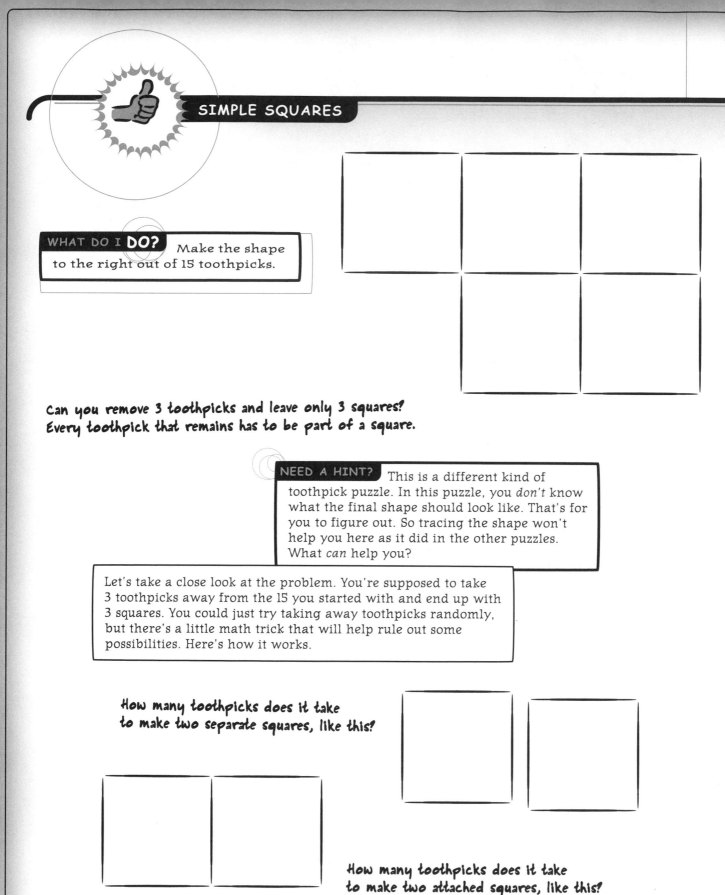

Once you take away 3 toothpicks, there'll be 12 toothpicks left. You have to make 3 squares with them. That means there are 4 toothpicks available for each square. What *that* means is that the solution you want must be made of separate squares. You know that the squares in the solution don't share any walls.

The solution is on page 135.

WHAT'S DIFFERENT ABOUT THESE TOOTHPICK PUZZLES?

Some people find it easier to do puzzles like this one, where the toothpicks fit together in geometric shapes instead of forming animals. That's because you're less likely to make assumptions about a simple shape. You're not worried about keeping the goat's feet on the ground or turning a fish's head into a tail fin.

The math trick you used to help you with this puzzle can be used to help you solve the rest of the puzzles in this chapter. Just divide the number of toothpicks you have by the number of shapes you're supposed to make.

If the result is the same as the number of toothpicks that you need to make that shape (4 for a square, 3 for a triangle), then you know that the shapes will be separate and won't share walls. If the result is less than the number of toothpicks you'd need to make that shape, then there must be shared walls. The rest is up to you!

Here are 4 more puzzles that are a lot like "Simple Squares." Give them a try!

SLIGHTLY LESS SIMPLE SQUARES

WHAT DO I **DO?** Make this shape out of 12 toothpicks.

Can you move 4 toothpicks around to make 3 squares?

Remember, you have to move the toothpicks, not remove them. And each toothpick has to be part of a square.

There are several different solutions to this puzzle. Some of them are on page 136.

TRICKY TRIANGLES

WHAT DO I DO? Use 16 toothpicks to make this shape.

Can you take away 4 toothpicks so there are 4 identical triangles left?

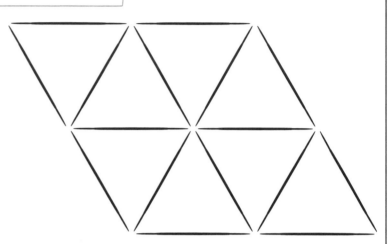

One solution is on page 136.

NOT-AT-ALL SIMPLE SQUARES

WHAT DO I DO? Make this shape out of 15 toothpicks.

Can you move 2 toothpicks to make 5 identical squares?

The solution is on page 136.

TRIANGLE CHALLENGE

WHAT DO I DO? This one is a little harder. Start with the shape below, using 9 toothpicks.

Move 4 toothpicks to make 5 triangles.

Here's a hint:
The triangles won't all be the same size.

One solution is on page 136.

SEEING SOLUTIONS

Whether you're struggling with a puzzle or a real-life problem, every once in a while the solution will just pop out at you, and you'll suddenly see it. A fancy word for seeing possible solutions in your head is "visualization." When you're trying to solve problems that involve putting things together or arranging things, visualization can be a really powerful tool.

Suppose you decided to take apart your bicycle, but then you couldn't remember how it went together. If you looked carefully at each part, you might notice that some of the parts just *look* like they fit together. Even better, you could have drawn a picture of how the parts fit together as you were taking the bike apart.

As you may have found out with some of these puzzles, drawing pictures can help you see solutions that don't "pop out" at you right away. Just the act of drawing a picture can help you notice things that otherwise you might have missed.

WHAT NOW?

If you want to play around with how your assumptions can get in your way when you're solving problems, go to **Through the Trapdoor** on page 98.

If you like taking shapes apart and putting them together in new ways, go to the **Temple of Tan** on page 82.

If you want to continue to explore the **Puzzle House,** turn the page to enter the **Logic Lounge.**

4

"When you have eliminated the impossible, whatever remains must be the truth."

-Sherlock Holmes

Detectives Needed!

Within this room are many mysteries to be unraveled.

If your powers of observation are keen, and you're good at putting clues together, you may enter.

Logical thinking is the only tool you need.

PUZZLE POLICE LINE - DO NOT CROSS

LINE - DO NOT CRO

Unsolved Cases

UNSOLVED CASES

These logic puzzles start out easy and get harder. To solve each case, read the story and figure out the answer to the question that's posed. Along the way, the Science-at-Home team has provided tips that will help you figure out how to solve these mysterious puzzles. But even with our tips, the last puzzle will be a challenge.

THE CASE OF THE MESSY ROOM

It's Matt's birthday. His sister Heather bought a present for him and slipped it under his door. But Matt hasn't cleaned his room in a while, and there are 10 things on the floor.

Can you figure out which of these things is Matt's birthday present?

Things on Matt's Floor:

dill pickle
bowling ball
library book
Spiderman comic book
cheese sandwich

five-dollar bill
Matt's report card
pancake
watermelon
football helmet

Clues:
A. The birthday gift was not green.
B. The gift was not something to eat.

TIPS FOR SOLVING LOGIC PUZZLES

LOOK FOR THE IMPOSSIBLE

If you know for sure that something is not true, you can eliminate it. When you know that it's impossible for an item to be Matt's birthday present, cross it off the list.

READ EVERYTHING VERY CAREFULLY

The clues in a logic puzzle, as in any puzzle or detective story, are written to be a little tricky.

Turn the page for more help solving this puzzle.

HELP! I'M STUMPED! Well, what's impossible? You know the gift isn't green, so you can cross the pickle, the watermelon, and the five-dollar bill off the list. You also know the gift wasn't food—there goes the cheese sandwich and the pancake.

What else do you know? Read everything—including the introduction—very, very carefully. Ah ha! It says that Heather *bought* the present, so you know it can't be Matt's report card or the library book. But that still leaves 3 possible presents.

With only 3 things left, you might be tempted to guess which one's the present. But in a logic puzzle, you *never* have to guess. All the clues are there to tell you which solution *has* to be the correct one.

So take one more look. Is anything else impossible? Yes! It also says that Heather slipped the present *under the door*. That means the gift can't be the bowling ball or the football helmet. So the only thing that's left on the list *must* be Matt's birthday present—a Spiderman comic book.

THE CASE OF THE BAFFLING BIKES

Three kids—Megan Brown, Rosie White, and Rachel Green—just got new mountain bikes. Each bike is the same color as one of the girls' last names.

MEGAN: "THAT'S WEIRD, OUR BIKES MATCH OUR LAST NAMES, BUT NONE OF US HAS A BIKE THAT MATCHES HER OWN NAME!"

GIRL WITH THE GREEN BIKE: "SO WHAT?"

What color is each girl's bike?

use the grid on the next page to help solve this puzzle.

MORE TIPS FOR SOLVING LOGIC PUZZLES

LOOK FOR RELATIONSHIPS BETWEEN CLUES

No one's bike matches her name, so you know that the girl with the brown bike can't be Megan Brown.

ORGANIZE THE INFORMATION YOU HAVE

Use this grid to keep track of what's true and what's not. If it's impossible for Megan to have the brown bike, put an ✗ in the square where "Megan" and "brown bike" intersect. When you find out something that is true, put a • in that square. Always use pencil when you are filling out a grid. That way, you can erase your mistakes. Better yet, make a photocopy of the page and use the photocopy!

	BROWN BIKE	WHITE BIKE	GREEN BIKE
MEGAN BROWN	✗		
ROSIE WHITE			
RACHEL GREEN			

The solution and the steps to solving the puzzle are on pages 136–137.

THE CASE OF THE MIXED-UP CARS

Lenny, Andrew, Daniel, and Ben have just finished a soccer game. Ben's mom and Daniel's dad are picking their boys up, and Lenny is getting a ride home with Andrew's brother. When they get to the parking lot, there are three cars—a Jeep Cherokee, a Datsun, and a Volvo. Lenny asks which car belongs to Andrew's family, but his friends give him confusing answers.

> MY MOM'S PARKED NEXT TO THE JEEP CHEROKEE.

BEN

> HEY, THAT'S OUR OLD DATSUN! WE SOLD IT WHEN WE GOT OUR NEW CAR

> THE DATSUN'S NEXT TO MY DAD'S CAR.

DANIEL

Can you help Lenny figure out which car belongs to each family?

(The order that the cars are listed in the grid isn't necessarily the order in which the cars are parked.)

See page 114 for more tips.

If you get stuck, see page 137 for the solution.

	JEEP	DATSUN	VOLVO
BEN'S MOM			
DANIEL'S DAD			
ANDREW'S BROTHER			

MORE TIPS FOR SOLVING LOGIC PUZZLES

MORE ABOUT GRIDS

Only one square in each row or column can have a •, because only one combination is true. Once you have a • in a square, you can put **X**s in all the other squares in that row and in that column. In complicated puzzles, this will help you see what's possible and what's not.

There can only be one • in any row or any column.
Once you've put a • in a column, you can also put Xs
in all the other squares in the same row as the •.

READ THE CLUES AGAIN

Once you've gone through all the clues and filled in the **X**s and •s that you know, you may feel stuck. Go back and read each clue again, carefully. Chances are you'll discover a piece of information that you missed the first time, and then you can solve the puzzle.

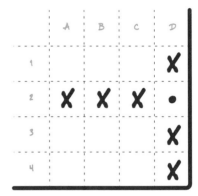

ONE MORE TIP FOR SOLVING LOGIC PUZZLES

Here's a tip that will help you solve "The Case of the Perplexing Performers" on the next page.

LOOK FOR RELATIONSHIPS

This is a much harder puzzle. There are 3 different ways to match up information: kid/month, kid/act, and act/month. That's why this grid looks different, and why the months are listed twice.

One clue may tell you that one kid didn't perform in a particular month. Another clue may connect that same month with an act, but not with a specific kid. You'll need to make all 3 kinds of connections to solve the puzzle.

THE CASE OF THE PERPLEXING PERFORMERS

Each month, one of the kids in the sixth grade class at Baker Street School does a performance for the rest of the class. So far this year, 5 different kids have done 5 different acts. Use the clues below to see if you can figure out the month that each kid performed (one of the kids is Simon), and what they performed (one kid played the accordion).

Clues:

1. Gregory's magnificent piano solo was not the act in January.

2. Katey performed in October.

3. The rap singer, who was not Brandon, entertained the class in December.

4. September's show featured the juggler.

5. Marika got a standing ovation for her magic tricks.

	GREGORY	BRANDON	KATEY	MARIKA	SIMON	SEPTEMBER	OCTOBER	NOVEMBER	DECEMBER	JANUARY
MAGIC TRICKS										
ACCORDION										
JUGGLING										
PIANO										
RAP SINGING										
SEPTEMBER					
OCTOBER					
NOVEMBER					
DECEMBER					
JANUARY					

With a puzzle this complicated, it's a good idea to make a photocopy before you start. That way if you get your Xs and •s confused, you'll have another blank grid to work with.

If you get stuck, see page 137 for the solution.

There has been a rash of thefts in Science City. Five items have been stolen (the solid gold bar was the 2nd), and the police know that 5 different crooks (one of them is Bad Betsy) are involved. So the city has hired 5 famous detectives to solve the crimes. (One of them is Jessica Fletcher, who caught the final crook.)

Using the clues in the introduction and below, can you figure out the item that each crook stole, the detective who caught each crook, and the order in which the crooks were caught?

Clues:

1. Mad Martha stole the secret formula.

2. Tommy Trouble was caught right after the crook who stole the briefcase, who was nabbed immediately after Inspector Gadget got his man.

3. Sticky Ricky was the 3rd crook caught.
Miss Marple was the 1st detective to catch a thief.

4. Nancy Drew caught the jewel thief.

5. The crook who stole the Nobel Prize was caught immediately before Willy the Weasel, who was nabbed right before Encyclopedia Brown caught a criminal.

6. Willy the Weasel didn't take anyone's briefcase.

Whoa. This one is really hard. There are 6 different relationships (detective/order, detective/loot, detective/crook, crook/order, crook/loot, and loot/order), which is why the grid on the next page has 6 different sections where things intersect.

The solution is on pages 137–138. Tips for solving this one are on page 118.

Read everything very carefully.

Look for the impossible.

	INSPECTOR GADGET	ENCYCLOPEDIA BROWN	MISS MARPLE	JESSICA FLETCHER	NANCY DREW	RICKY	MARTHA	TOMMY	BETSY	WILLY	FORMULA	BRIEFCASE	JEWELS	GOLD	NOBEL PRIZE
1ST															
2ND															
3RD															
4TH															
5TH															
FORMULA															
BRIEFCASE															
JEWELS															
GOLD															
NOBEL PRIZE															
RICKY															
MARTHA															
TOMMY															
BETSY															
WILLY															

Organize the information you have.

	DETECTIVE	CROOK	LOOT
1ST			
2ND			
3RD			
4TH			
5TH			

Read the clues carefully.

FILLING IN INFORMATION

Go through all the clues and fill in all the •s you can. Remember, anytime you put a • in a section, you can put **X**s in the rest of that row and column—but only in that one *section*.

ORDER IS VERY IMPORTANT

In this puzzle, events happened in a particular order. Take a look at clue #2. It doesn't tell you anything for sure, but it does tell you a whole lot about what's impossible.

- You know that Tommy did not steal the briefcase (he was caught after that crook), and you also know he wasn't caught by Inspector Gadget (that was *before* the guy with the briefcase, and Tommy was caught after).
- You also know that Inspector Gadget did not catch the guy with the briefcase or catch Tommy.
- So you can put **X**s in all those boxes (Gadget/briefcase, Gadget/Tommy, Tommy/briefcase, etc.)

What else do you know from this clue? If you read carefully, you'll discover that 3 crooks were caught in this order:

Inspector **Gadget's** man
    The crook who stole the **Briefcase**
Tommy Trouble

Ah ha! It's impossible for Tommy to be the 1st or 2nd crook caught. Two crooks were caught before him, so the earliest he can be is 3rd. Write down the possibilities from this clue on a piece of scrap paper:

Gadget 1 2 3 (he could be 1st, 2nd, or 3rd)
Briefcase 2 3 4 (he could be 2nd, 3rd, or 4th)
Tommy 3 4 5 (he could be 3rd, 4th, or 5th)

DON'T FORGET: LOOK FOR THE IMPOSSIBLE

When you eliminate one possibility, you can also eliminate some of the others. For example, in clue #3, you discover that Miss Marple was the 1st detective to catch a crook. So it's *not* possible for Inspector Gadget to be 1st. That means that the briefcase (which happened right after Gadget) can't be 2nd, and Tommy (who was caught right after the briefcase), can't be 3rd. Now your list looks like this:

Gadget X 2 3
Briefcase X 3 4
Tommy X 4 5

Through the information in other clues, you'll be able to eliminate one of these remaining possibilities. Then you'll know for sure what position Gadget, the briefcase, and Tommy occupy. You can put •s in the grid, fill in some big gaps in the table, and the rest of the puzzle will begin to fall into place.

USE THE TABLE

This is a complicated puzzle. You'll need two kinds of charts to keep track of the information—a grid and a table. Once you've filled in the grid with dozens of **X**s and lots of •s, it can look very confusing. The table helps you see exactly what information you're missing.

You know from clue #3 that Sticky Ricky was the 3rd crook caught. So you can write "Ricky" in the 3rd row of the table, under CROOK (see below). When you finally link Ricky up with a detective, you can write the detective's name in the table next to "Ricky." And that will remind you that detective must be 3rd, too, because he caught Ricky.

Some information won't go in the table right away. You know that Mad Martha took the secret formula, so you can connect those 2 things in the grid. But you can't put them in the table yet, because you haven't discovered *when* Martha was captured. You might want to write down "Martha-formula" on scrap paper so that when you can put them in the table, you'll remember.

KEEP MAKING CONNECTIONS

There are lots and lots of ways that information is linked together in this puzzle. You know that Ricky was caught 3rd. Let's say you find out that it's impossible for him to have stolen a particular piece of loot. If it's not Ricky's loot, *it* can't be 3rd. So you get to put another **X** in the grid.

This is a very, very tricky puzzle. Read each clue over carefully. You may go back and read some of them 3 or 4 times before you pull out the last little fact you need.

WHAT NOW?

If you like solving puzzles that seem impossible at first, try **Through the Trapdoor** on page 98.

If you like figuring out how lots of different pieces fit together, try the **Temple of Tan** on page 82.

If you like filling grids with **X**s, visit the **Grotto of Games** on page 60.

If you like figuring out how to organize the clues in logic puzzles, check out "Get Organized!" in the **Lost and Found** on page 23.

If you want to continue to explore the **Puzzle House,** turn the page.

BEGINNINGS

Each of these puzzles is a familiar phrase, the title of a book, or a song, or a movie, perhaps even a famous quote. Each contains a number, some words, and some initials, the beginnings of other words. The numbers are clues to help you figure out what word each initial stands for. Your challenge is to figure out the rest of the missing words.

Take a look at this one: **26. L. in the A.**

It "translates" to   **26 letters in the alphabet**

Take a look at the puzzles on this page and the next. You may figure some of them out quickly, but you may get stuck on others. Don't give up right away. Give your brain plenty of time to play around with the possibilities. The Science-at-Home team has provided some tips about ways to crack open a puzzle that has you stumped. And the solutions to all the puzzles are on page 138.

THE STARTING LINE

WHAT DO I DO? Figure out which words are missing, using the numbers and initials as clues.

50 S. in the U.

9 P. in the S. S.

16 O. in a P.

365 D. in a Y.

52 W. in a Y.

10 Y. in a D.

101 D.

5 D. in a Z. C.

24 H. in a D.

7 C. in the R.

TIPS FOR SOLVING THIS KIND OF PUZZLE

SAY IT OUT LOUD

Sometimes, you get the answer right away. It just pops out at you. But if it doesn't just pop, don't keep staring at the letters. Try saying the puzzle out loud. Sometimes hearing the number is enough of a clue for your brain to remember the rest of the phrase.

PLAY WITH THE NUMBERS

Some numbers, like 3, or 5, or 10, have many different things connected to them. Lots of things come in 3s. There are 3 feet in a yard, 3 wheels on a tricycle, 3 little pigs in the fairy tale, and so on. If the puzzle has a small or common number in it, list all the things you can think of that involve that number, and you may hit something with the right initials.

More tips are on the next page.

With other numbers, like 365, only one possibility is likely. If you can't think of it right away, just play around with the number—say it out loud or write it down. If you keep fooling around, sooner or later your brain is likely to remember where it's heard that number before.

PLAY WITH THE LETTERS

If you're still stumped, try thinking of all the words you know that begin with one of the letters in the puzzle. Say the words out loud as you think of them. Ellen of the Science-at-Home team says that when she can't think of the exact word, making sounds that are close to it often gives her brain enough clues to come up with the solution.

TAKE A BREAK

If you're really, really stuck, the best thing to do is stop trying so hard and go do something else for a while. Sometimes the word you're trying to remember will pop into your head when you're not thinking about it.

MORE BAFFLING BEGINNINGS

You may need the tips that start on page 121 when you try to solve the rest of these puzzles. The first batch is a little difficult, and the last ones may be a challenge even for the most serious puzzle masters!

1 W. on a U.

4 Q. in a F. G.

5 N. in a Q.

8 S. on a S. S.

12 S. of the Z.

13 S. on the A. F.

18 H. on a G. C.

64 S. on a C. B.

88 K. on a P.

90 D. in a R. A.

1001 A. N.

20,000 L. under the S.

Remember, if you can't figure out a puzzle right away, don't give up. Take a break and keep that pesky puzzle in the back of your mind. You may come up with the solution when you least expect it. Something you hear or say can trigger a connection in your brain, and you'll have one of those surprising—and satisfying—"ah ha!" moments.

COMPLETELY CONFOUNDING CONUNDRUMS

1 S. S. for M., 1 G. L. for M.

2 W. D'nt M. a R.

3 B. M. (S. H. T. R. !)

7 D. in S. W.

10 F. in a G. of B.

1,000 W. that a P. is W.

24 B. B. B. in a P.

76 T. L. the B. P.

99 B. of B. on the W.

200 D. for P. G. in M.

WHERE DID THESE PUZZLES COME FROM?

In 1981, a puzzle creator named Will Shortz printed 24 of these short puzzles in an issue of Games magazine. He called them "language equations," because they had both letters and numbers in them. People sent in dozens more, some of which were printed in the magazine. Today, there are hundreds of these intriguing word puzzles around. People are making new ones up every day—and you can, too!

MAKING YOUR OWN PUZZLES

Make your own puzzles and perplex your pals.

WHAT DO I **DO?**

Find a number—like how many feet in a mile. Write it down: **5280 Feet in a Mile**

Now abbreviate the words so that they're just initials. Leave little words like "in" and "a" as they are. You'll end up with this puzzle to try on your friends or family: **5280 F. in a M.**

That one's pretty simple. The number 5,280 is usually only connected to one thing. You can make your puzzles as easy or as hard as you want.

You can find numbers to use in many different places. Measurements are good. Some fairy tales have numbers in them. So do some old sayings, like "a stitch in time saves 9." And there are lots of numbers connected with various sports and games. Take a look around and see what you can find.

You can even use numbers that apply just to your family, like birthdates, or how many boys (or girls) there are, or your street address. Those puzzles will be really special, because only people in your family can solve them.

WHAT NOW?

If you like playing with words, go to the **Plexer Studio** on page 92 or **Leak Lake** on page 54.

If you like having the first letter and thinking of the rest of the word, learn about how this can help you remember things at **Treasure Chest** on page 34.

Can't quite think of a word? Want to know why? Go to **Lost and Found** on page 18.

If you like having part of a problem, and having to fill in the rest, go to **Jumping the Gap** on page 48.

If you want to continue to explore the **Puzzle House,** turn the page.

THERE'S MORE THAN ONE ANSWER...

A lot of the puzzles and problems in these notebooks have had one solution. There's been a "right answer." But in real life, there may not be just one solution to a problem. You may be able to solve it in many different ways.

In these activities, your challenge is to see how many different ways you can think of to solve the same problem. You'll need to be creative.

WHAT ARE CREATIVE PEOPLE REALLY LIKE?

Here are some of the ways you can recognize another creative person.

CREATIVE PEOPLE TRY UNEXPECTED METHODS.

CREATIVE PEOPLE TRY NEW THINGS.

CREATIVE PEOPLE FEEL LIKE THEY CAN CHANGE THE WORLD.

CREATIVE PEOPLE KNOW HOW TO JOKE AND PLAY.

CREATIVE PEOPLE WORK TOWARD A GOAL.

CREATIVE PEOPLE LIKE TO EXPERIMENT.

CREATIVE PEOPLE PAY ATTENTION TO THE PEOPLE AND STUFF AROUND THEM.

CREATIVE PEOPLE STRIKE OUT IN THEIR OWN DIRECTION. THEY DON'T FOLLOW THE CROWD.

CREATIVE PEOPLE ARE WILLING TO MAKE A MESS.

CREATIVE PEOPLE TAKE RISKS.

CREATIVE PEOPLE ARE WILLING TO CHANGE.

CREATIVE PEOPLE DON'T MIND WHEN THE ANSWERS AREN'T NEAT AND TIDY.

CREATIVE PEOPLE KEEP TRYING EVEN AFTER THEY FAIL.

CREATIVE PEOPLE DON'T MIND WHEN THINGS GET COMPLICATED.

CREATIVE PEOPLE FEEL LIKE THEY KNOW WHAT THEY'RE DOING MOST OF THE TIME.

CREATIVE PEOPLE DON'T LIMIT THEMSELVES TO JUST ONE ANSWER.

CREATIVE PEOPLE DON'T WORRY ABOUT WHAT EVERYONE ELSE WILL THINK.

CREATIVE PEOPLE ARE BRAVE.

CREATIVE PEOPLE ARE CURIOUS.

MAKING CONNECTIONS

WHAT DO I DO?

1. Take a look at these 3 words:

BANANA   CHEESECAKE   JELLY

How are the words connected to each other? They're all foods. They're all sweet. They're all words that use at least one letter twice. There are lots of different answers.

2. Now look at the groups of words below. You might think the words don't have much in common with each other. But is that true, or is that an assumption you made at first glance?

3. Take some time and see what connections you can discover. Try 3 words in one row, 4 words in a column, or close your eyes and pick any 3 words to connect together.

BALLOON	FOOTBALL	JELLY
ROSE	CLOCK	RABBIT
TELEPHONE	RAISIN	MIRROR
OSTRICH	BASKET	POPCORN

Turn the page to try more connections.

MAKING YOUR OWN CONNECTIONS Make your own lists of words by closing your eyes and opening the dictionary (or the phone book, or a cookbook, or any old book you pull off the shelf). Put your finger down on the page that fell open. Write down the word your finger touched. Do this until you have a list of random, unrelated words. How many ways can you find to connect them together? This is a fun game to play around a table with some friends.

WHY AM I DOING THIS? This is an exercise in creative thinking. Putting things together in a brand new way is one method for getting your mind out of a rut. Many problems have been solved by creative thinkers who made connections no one had ever thought of before.

FOUND POETRY

If you liked making connections with single words, try making poems by collecting bits and pieces from newspapers, magazines, and books.

WHAT DO I NEED? • A magazine or newspaper that no one will mind if you cut up.
• Scissors
• Paper
• Tape

WHAT DO I DO? **1.** Read the newspaper or magazine until you find a sentence or group of words that you like. Cut those words out. Then start reading again until you find another sentence or group of words that you like. Cut those out, too. Keep on going until you have more than a dozen sentences or groups of words.

2. Take all words you've cut out and lay them out on a blank piece of paper. They probably don't make much sense when you first look at them. Do any of them seem to go together? Put those groups of words together and see how you like that.

3. Rearrange the words until you have something that feels like a poem to you. You don't have to use all the words. You can leave some sentences out or cut words out of some sentences. But you can't add any words. Your poem doesn't have to make much sense. It doesn't have to rhyme. It can be funny if you like.

4. You can add punctuation if you like. Put in commas and periods where you need them.

5. Tape all the sentences down on the page and share your poem with your family and friends.

WHAT THE SCIENCE-AT-HOME TEAM DID The Science-at-Home expedition photocopied pages from an old book about science for kids and found poetry hidden among its sentences.

ANNIE DILLARD

Pulitzer Prize–winning author Annie Dillard wrote a book of poetry called Mornings Like This. Well, she didn't actually write it. She found all the pieces of it and put them together. She took some otherwise uninteresting books (an old textbook, a navigator's handbook, a first-aid book, the instructions that came with a set of watercolor paints) and used the sentences in them to make poems.

Magic That Flows

The children watched
   as strange things happened.
Holes appeared in every room,
Fastened to electric cords.
The children could not wait
   until dark.
The mother rushed through the room:
What was it like?

In this poem, we used the sentences in the order that we found them on the page. There were lots of other words in between the sentences we used. But we didn't want **those** words for our poem, so we left them out.

OBJECT MASQUERADE

Here's a fun party game to play with your creative friends.

WHAT DO I **DO?**

Put a dozen objects in a bag. Have everyone stand in a circle. The first person pulls an object out of the bag, and pretends that it's something else. She might talk into a shoe, making it a telephone. She might cradle it in her arms and sing a lullaby, pretending the shoe is a baby.

Pass the object around the circle until everyone has turned it into something different. Then have another person pick a new object out of the bag and continue. You'll be exercising your creative thinking—and laughing a lot, we promise.

WHAT NOW?

If you want to see how making connections can help you remember, go to **Base Camp** on page 10, **Combination Cave** on page 26, or **Lost and Found** on page 18.

If you want to work your ability to make connections to solve a mystery, visit **Logic Lounge** on page 110.

If you want to play more games with other people, go to **Leak Lake** on page 54, **Grotto of Games** on page 60, or **Jumping the Gap** on page 48.

If you want to play with words, check out the **Plexer Studio** on page 92.

If you want to exercise your creativity by inventing your own puzzles, visit the **Temple of Tan** on page 82, **Cave Paintings** on page 30, or "Jumping to Conclusions" in **Jumping the Gap** on page 49.

This is the last notebook, but that doesn't mean your journey is over. You can make up your own puzzles, write your own notebooks, and revisit places you've already explored.

Keep on exploring the world inside your head!

HOW TO BE A GOOD PUZZLE AND PROBLEM SOLVER

GET AN ATTITUDE

The first step in solving a problem is having the right attitude.

Be Confident.

Don't be afraid to try.

Relax. Take your time.

Don't get discouraged. If you don't figure it out right away, try again. Or move on to something else for a while.

Be Creative.

Some of the attitudes of creative people are noted on page 125.

GET OUT OF YOUR OWN WAY

You've got a problem and you still can't find a solution. Here are some of the ways you could be making the problem harder for yourself.

Take another look!

You're seeing what you expect to see, not what's really there. Take another look!

You're following habits or rules that may not apply to this problem. Do something unexpected!

Do something unexpected!

You're afraid you're going to try something and look silly. Get over it! Brilliant ideas sometimes come from silly beginnings.

Get over it!

Brilliant ideas sometimes come from silly beginnings.

TRY A DIFFERENT APPROACH

There's an old saying that if all you have is a hammer, you treat everything like a nail. If you only know one way of solving problems, you'll just hammer away, trying to solve everything that way. A lot of the time, that won't work.

Puzzles are just like other problems: There are lots of ways to solve them. A method may work great for solving one problem but not help you at all with another. That's why it's important to try different approaches when you're solving problems. The more tricks you have up your sleeve, the more likely you are to find a solution.

Even the best problem solvers get stuck. Here are some ideas that you can try to get yourself unstuck.

Look at the problem from a different viewpoint. Turn it upside down—or stand on your head.

Use another one of your senses. You could draw a picture of the problem, say it out loud, or organize all the information you've got in a new way.

Think about other problems you've solved. Maybe one of them is like this one.

Get someone else to help. Talk about the problem with a friend. Maybe he or she will see something that you missed—or just have a different perspective.

Take inventory.

Take inventory. What do you have? What do you know? What do you need?

Ask a lot of questions.

Never assume.

Never assume. Think about lots and lots of possible answers before you decide that anything is impossible.

Question the ordinary way of doing things. Pretend you're from another planet and you don't know anything about how things usually work. Can you see an unexpected solution?

If you get stuck, take a break. You aren't being lazy. Psychologists who study problem solving say that taking a break can help you get rid of stuff that's getting in your way.

Watch out for traps you set for yourself.

Don't just do the same thing over and over again. Try something new.

Is there a simpler version of the same problem? Solve that one first!

Eliminate the impossible. What do you have left?

Break a big problem into smaller steps.

Look ahead! What are you planning to do? What will happen if you do that? Do you have any other choices?

Look ahead!

Look back!

Look back! If the problem has you stumped, think about what the solution needs to be. Where do you need to end up? What are some possible steps that would lead from there back to where you are?

Look for patterns.

Look at the solution. Not right away, but if you get too frustrated, you're not having fun. No one can solve every puzzle. The solution to this puzzle may give you an idea about how to solve the next one.

Play with it. Have a good time!

ABOUT YOUR BRAIN

On your travels through the Caverns of Memory, the Forest of Hidden Surprises, and the Puzzle House, you've been exploring what you can do with that brain of yours. It's kind of amazing—a few pounds of stuff in your skull lets you read these words, draw a picture, solve a puzzle, develop a strategy to win at Tic-Tac-Toe, or throw a baseball. How does your brain manage all that?

Scientists studying the brain have figured out which parts of the brain move muscles, control the blinking of your eyelids, or tell your heart to beat. These are some of the basic body functions that your brain controls. But scientists have also figured out which sections of your brain recognize patterns, identify the names of smells, sights, and sounds, or make plans. What parts of your brain have you been using in the Caverns of Memory, the Forest of Hidden Surprises, and the Puzzle House?

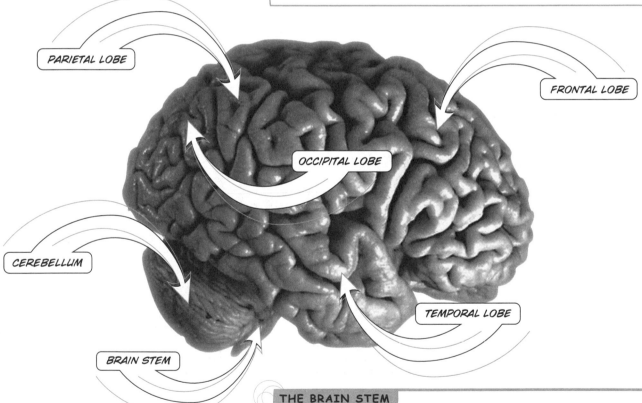

PARIETAL LOBE

FRONTAL LOBE

OCCIPITAL LOBE

CEREBELLUM

TEMPORAL LOBE

BRAIN STEM

THE BRAIN STEM

Keeping You Alive. Deep inside your brain, there is an area responsible for the basic body functions you need to stay alive. In this part of the brain, called the "brain stem," you'll find the "medulla," "midbrain," and "pons." The "medulla" controls your heartbeat, breathing, and blood pressure. It also triggers sneezing, coughing, hiccuping, and vomiting. The "midbrain" controls certain basic eye movements, like blinking and focusing. The "pons" lies between the medulla and midbrain and helps send messages from the brain stem to other parts of your brain.

heartbeat coughing
breathing hiccuping
blood pressure vomiting
sneezing blinking
focusing

THE HIPPOCAMPUS AND THALAMUS

The Memory Center. There are two sections of the brain that lie near the brain stem: the "hippocampus" and "thalamus." Both help you form certain kinds of memories.

Your "hippocampus" forms memories of names and events that don't need to be repeated to be remembered. For example, if you got straight As on your last report card, your hippocampus would create that memory for you and another part of your brain would store it. Your "thalamus," on the other hand, also stores memories, but only for a very short time. These are memories that you use for less than a minute or so, and then they are either forgotten or stored in other parts of the brain for later use. For example, your thalamus helps you remember the string of words you need to finish a sentence or the numbers you need to telephone a friend. (You use both your hippocampus and thalamus as you wander through the Caverns of Memory.)

THE CEREBRAL CORTEX

It's All Happening on the Outside. The word "cortex" comes from the Latin work for "bark." That's because the cerebral cortex is a thin, outer layer of tissue that covers the brain just like bark covers the trunk of a tree. Even though this layer is very thin, it's this part of the brain that lets you think, sense things, and be creative. There are four parts of the cortex, called "lobes," that you use as you do the experiments and puzzles in this book. These lobes are the "frontal lobe," "parietal lobe," "occipital lobe," and "temporal lobe."

"memory"

THE FRONTAL LOBE

The Planning Center. Your frontal lobe is responsible for making mental pictures of the world and for retrieving complex memories. It's also where memories of smell and emotions related to smell are stored. Another part of the frontal lobe is responsible for creativity and problem solving. You'll use this part of your brain wherever you wander in this book!

THE PARIETAL LOBE

Center For Touch, Pain, and Body Position. Sensations and memories of touch, pain, temperature, and body position are received and analyzed here. The back of the parietal lobe helps you locate the position of your body parts in space.

THE OCCIPITAL LOBE

Center For Seeing and Visual Perception. The occipital lobe analyzes the signals that come from your eyes. It's in this part of the brain that you put together information about the visual world around you. When you perceive color, motion, or shape, you're using this part of your brain. (You can challenge your occipital lobe with the visual illusions in Trickery Thicket on page 68 and the Garden of Illusions on page 76.)

THE TEMPORAL LOBE

Center For Stored Memories. Memories of things you've heard and seen are stored here. You use your temporal lobe to identify familiar sounds and comprehend what people are saying to you. The temporal lobe also helps you recognize familiar visual patterns, like the faces of your family members. (When you wander through the Forest of Hidden Surprises, you give this part of your brain a real workout.)

THE CEREBELLUM

Center For Planning and Executing Motion. In the back of your head, where your neck meets your head, there is a part of the brain called the "cerebellum." The word "cerebellum" comes from the Latin for "little brain." The cerebellum is actually a pair of organs, each made up of folded tissue and about the size of a golf ball. This part of the brain controls movement, balance, and coordination. Memories involving the position of different body parts are stored here. Without the cerebellum, you wouldn't be able to remember how to walk, ride a bike, throw a ball, or play a musical instrument.

SOLUTIONS

2. Lost and Found (pages 18–25)

• Common Cents
G is the right penny.

• A Is for Apple, B Is for Crab
Fruit beginning with the letter **P? Pear**
Animal beginning with . . . **D? Deer**
Metal beginning with . . . **I? Iron**
Bird beginning with . . . **B? Bluebird**
Country beginning with . . . **F? France**
Boy's name beginning with . . . **H? Harold**
Girl's name beginning with . . . **P? Pamela**
Vegetable beginning with . . . **C? Carrot**
Sport beginning with . . . **S? Soccer**
Flower beginning with . . . **P? Pansy**

Fruit ending with . . . **H? Peach**
Animal ending with . . . **W? Cow**
Metal ending with . . . **R? Copper**
Bird ending with . . . **N? Wren**
Country ending with . . . **Y? Italy**
Boy's name ending with . . . **D? David**
Girl's name ending with . . . **N? Ellen**
Vegetable ending with . . . **T? Beet**
Sport ending with . . . **L? Baseball**
Flower ending with . . . **P? Tulip**

• I'm Thinking of...
• Colorful Surprise
Are you thinking of orange?
That's the color most people think of.

If you're thinking of orange, you probably thought of Denmark, one of the few countries with a name that begins with a D. (Our atlas also lists Djibouti, Dominica, and the Dominican Republic.) If you thought of Denmark, you needed to think of an animal beginning with a K. Chances are you thought of a kangaroo, since that's the most familiar animal beginning with K. If you thought of a kangaroo, then you had to think of a color that begins with O. Orange is the most common choice.

A few tricky people have managed to come up with other answers. If you think of a koala, then you'll have to come up with a color that begins with A, like aqua. Or if you think of a kiwi, you'll need a color that begins with I, like indigo. If you think of a kinkajou, you'll need a color that begins with U, like umber. But most people think of Denmark and a kangaroo.

You may want to use this trick to convince your friends that you can read minds!

• Adding Up Animals
Are you thinking of an elephant?
Most people do.

This trick is very sneaky. When you multiply any number between 1 and 10 by 9 and then add the digits, you get 9. Subtract 5 from 9 and you get 4. So when you count through the alphabet, you reach D. There's only one state, Delaware, that starts with a D. The second letter of Delaware is E.

And that's where memory comes in. If you ask most people to come up with an animal that begins with an E, they'll say "elephant." Sure, there are other animals that begin with E, like emu or echidna. But most of us grew up with alphabet books that had "E is for Elephant." So that's the first animal that comes to mind.

• Get Organized!
Here's how we organized the food list to make it easier to remember:

Food				
Snacks		**Meals**		
sweet	**salty**	**breakfast**	**lunch**	**dinner**
Snickers	potato chips	eggs	sandwich	meatloaf
Oreos	pretzels	toast	milk	potatoes
bubble gum	popcorn	cereal	apple	salad
Popsicle				carrots

4. Cave Paintings (pages 30–33)

• Droodles with Names
You might have had an easier time remembering the droodles if we'd called them by these names.

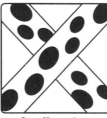

Giraffes in love

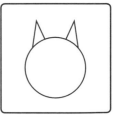

Rabbit blowing bubble

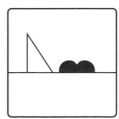

Shark returning from Walt Disney World

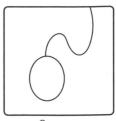

Bungee-jumping egg

1. Moonstruck on the Mountain (pages 42–47)

• Emoticons or Smileys

8)	Person wearing glasses
:-O	Surprised person
=I:)=	Abraham Lincoln
;-)	Person winking
:-P	Person sticking out tongue
****:-)	Marge Simpson

2. Jumping the Gap (pages 48–53)

• Jumping to Conclusions

Here are the letters that were under the black bar:

IUMRING TQ GQNGIUSIQNS

5. Trickery Thicket (pages 68–75)

• Double Trouble

If you've been puzzling over the pictures on page 70, here's some help. The picture at the top of the page can be either a saxophone player or a woman's face. If you're having trouble seeing the woman it may help to know that the little cloud below the saxophone player's nose is the woman's right eye.

The other picture is either a rat or a man with glasses. The rat's ears become the man's glasses. The tip of the nose is the same for both.

7. Temple of Tan (pages 82–89)

• Getting Warmed Up

• Tricky Triangle

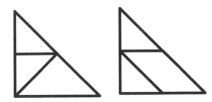

• Perplexing Polygon

• Make an Eagle

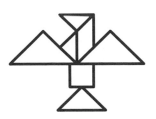

• More Tangrams to Try

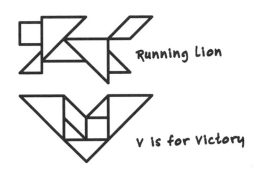

Running Lion

V Is for Victory

• Tangramania!

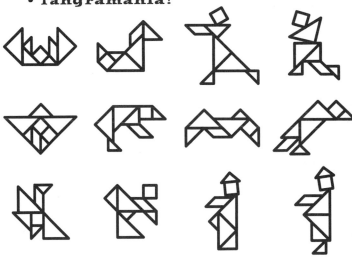

• Be Square

• Pat's Alien Tangram

1. Plexer Studio (pages 92–97)

• Some Perplexing Plexers
1. You're under arrest
2. Somewhere over the rainbow
3. Once upon a time
4. Rock around the clock
5. Tiptoe through the tulips
6. Looking backward

• More Plexers
7. Pineapple upside-down cake
8. Three square meals
9. 49ers (49 Rs)
10. I'm in the middle of something
11. Split pea
12. Broken promise
13. Railroad crossing
14. Any port in a storm

• Add a Colorful Touch
Encyclopedia Brown
Green thumb
Once in a blue moon

2. Through the Trapdoor
(pages 98–101)

• Never Assume Anything

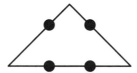

• One Word Answer
The solution? ONE WORD.

Some people think this is a cheat. "ONE WORD" is two words. But the puzzle didn't ask you to rearrange the letters into a *single* word. It asked you to rearrange them into *one* word. If you assumed that the solution had to be a single, 7-letter word, you got stuck.

• Tricky Toothpicks

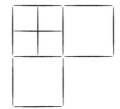

Some people think this solution cheats, too. That's because they thought all the squares had to be the same size. But that wasn't a rule. It was just an assumption.

• Trapped in the Terrible Joke Pit
1. The outside.
2. In the ground.
3. The numbers are in alphabetical order. (**ei**ght, **fi**ve, **fo**ur, **n**ine, **o**ne, **se**ven, **si**x, **th**ree, **tw**o, **z**ero)
4. Any ten-dollar bill is better than any one-dollar bill.
5. He weighs meat.
6. If you're looking at a clock. (Read it out loud. Ten to seven is the same as 6:50.)
7. No time at all. It's already been built.

• The Brain-Buster Stories
• All in the Family
The head physicist was the boy's mother.

• The River Rovers
It was winter. The creek was frozen, and they walked across.

• The Strange Race
Bill rode Jason's bike back to the playground. Bill's *bike* was the last to arrive, so Bill won.

• The Math Test
Jenny wrote down the equation 9 + 9 = 18. But Susan was sitting across the table, so Jenny's paper was upside down to her. Susan copied exactly what she saw, and wrote down: 81 = 6 + 6.

• The Jumping Horse
On a chessboard. The white knight was moved over the rook and landed on the square occupied by the black bishop, which was immediately removed from the board.

• It's in the Bag
It was Halloween.
Chris had gone trick-or-treating.

• Barnyard Baffler
The weather had gotten a lot warmer and Lisa's snowman had melted.

2. A Shift at the Snack Bar
(pages 102–109)

• Penny Triangle
This puzzle is simple once you notice that the group of 7 pennies in the middle is part of both the upright triangle and the upside-down triangle. Turning the triangle over is as easy as moving the 3 corners.

What makes this puzzle not-so-simple is that your instincts may be telling you to do something totally different. When you first think about this puzzle, you may notice that the triangle you start with has a row of 4 pennies at the bottom, and the triangle you need will have a row of 4 pennies at the top. So you may assume that these are the same 4 pennies, and they have to stay right where they are. But that messes you up, because 2 of these 4 *do* need to be moved (see diagram on the next page)...

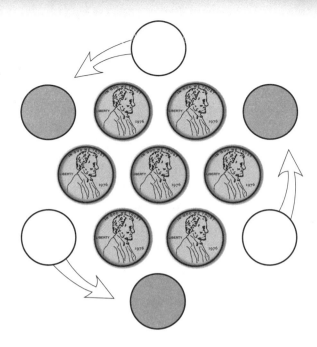

other part of the fish. If you can stop thinking of this group of toothpicks as a fish, and start looking at it as just a pattern, it's much easier to see the solution. Now see if you can figure out the other solution!

• Get Your Goat

To solve the puzzle, the toothpick that was the back becomes the front leg, and the toothpick that was the front leg becomes the back.

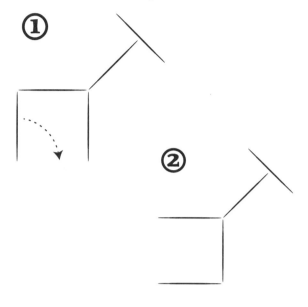

• Fish Flip

There are actually 2 ways to do it. Here's one. Move toothpicks 1, 2, and 3 from where they are in this drawing to where they are in the drawings below.

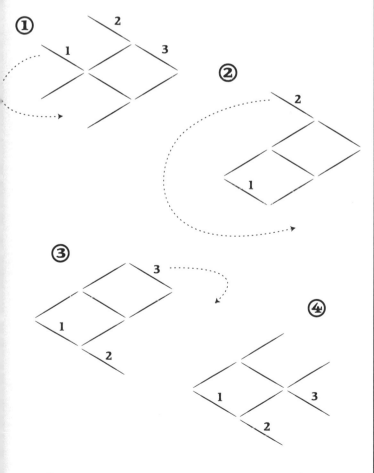

• Simple Squares

To leave 3 squares, take away the toothpicks numbered 1, 2, and 3.

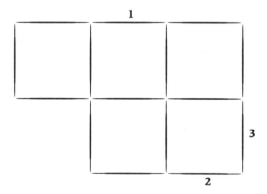

The only way to leave 3 whole squares is to take these 3 toothpicks away. As you can see, the remaining squares don't share any walls.

The assumption that can mess you up is that a fin has to stay a fin, and can't become some

• Slightly Less Simple Squares

There are lots of ways to get 3 squares. Here are 2 of them. Move toothpicks numbered 1, 2, 3, and 4.

(original)

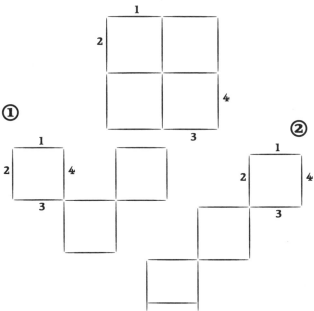

① ②

... to get this.

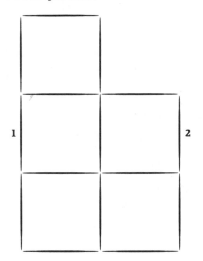

• Tricky Triangles

Take away these 4 toothpicks and you get 4 identical triangles.

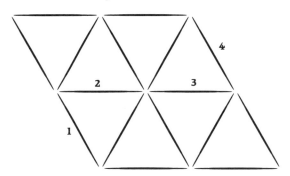

• Not-At-All Simple Squares

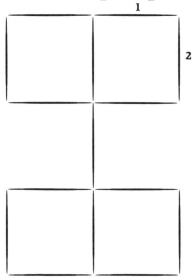

Move these two toothpicks . . .

• Triangle Challenge

Move these 4 . . .

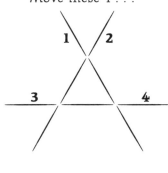

... to get this.

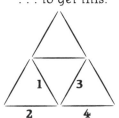

Do you see the fifth triangle? It's so big it holds the other 4!

4. Mysteries in the Logic Lounge
(pages 110–119)

• The Case of the Baffling Bikes

You know that Megan Brown can't have the brown bike. Is it impossible for her to have one of the other bikes? Yes! She can't have the green bike either, because the girl with the green bike is talking to Megan. That leaves Megan with the white bike.

How about Rachel Green? You know she can't have the green bike. And now you know she doesn't have the white bike either, because that one belongs to Megan. So Rachel must have the brown bike, and that leaves Rosie with the green one.

Megan • white bike

Rachel • brown bike

Rosie • green bike

• The Case of the Mixed-Up Cars

It's impossible for Ben's mom to be driving the Jeep, because she's parked next to it. It's also impossible for her to be driving the Datsun, because Ben's family sold that car. She has to be driving the Volvo.

So Daniel's dad isn't driving the Volvo. And since he's parked next to the Datsun, he's not driving that car either, which means he must be driving the Jeep. That leaves Andrew's brother behind the wheel of the Datsun.

Ben's Mom • Volvo

Daniel's Dad • Jeep

Andrew's Brother • Datsun

• The Case of the Perplexing Performers

Clue #1: Gregory played the piano •. All other kids get **X**s in the Piano row; Gregory gets **X**s in all other performance squares. Gregory did not perform in January (**X**) so the piano is not in January (**X**).

Clue #2: Katey performed in October •. All other kids get **X**s in October; Katey gets **X**s in all other months. Gregory played the piano, so the piano is not in October.

Clue #3: The singer is not Brandon (**X**). The singer performed in December •. All other performances get **X**s in December; Singing gets **X**s in all other months. Brandon gets an **X** in December. Katey's in October, so she gets an **X** in Singing.

Clue #4: The juggler was in September •. So all other performances get **X**s in September, and the juggler gets **X**s in all other months. And Katey gets an **X** in Juggling. The piano now has **X**s in every month except November, so the piano and Gregory both get •s in November. (Which means all other kids and all other performances get **X**s in November, too.)

Clue #5: Marika did magic •. So all other kids get **X**s in Magic, and Marika gets **X**s in all other performances. Now there's only one blank square in Singing row—Simon •. Singing is December, so Simon is December •. Marika has an **X** in October, so now Magic gets an **X** in October, which means Magic is January •. It also means the accordion is October •, so Katey played the accordion •, making Brandon the Juggler • and Brandon is in September •, which leaves Marika in January.

September • Juggler • Brandon

October • Accordion • Katey

November • Piano • Gregory

December • Rap Singer • Simon

January • Magic Tricks • Marika

• The Case of the 5 Crooks

Clues in introduction: gold bar is 2nd • —**X**s for all other loot at 2nd, and for gold in all other positions. Jessica Fletcher is 5th •; **X**s for Jessica at all other positions, and for all other detectives at 5th. **X** at gold/Jessica.

Clue #1: Martha/secret formula •. Martha **X**s all other loot; formula **X**s all other crooks. **X** at Martha/2nd.

Clue #2: **X**s at Tommy/1st, Tommy/2nd, Tommy/briefcase, Gadget/Tommy, Gadget/briefcase, Gadget/4th, briefcase/1st, briefcase/5th, Gadget/Betsy, Gadget/Martha (he catches his man).

Clue #3: • at Ricky/3rd. **X**s all other crooks for 3rd, **X**s all other positions for Ricky. • at Marple/1st. **X**s all other detectives for 1st, **X**s all other positions for Marple. **X**s at Marple/Ricky, Ricky/gold, Marple/gold, Marple/briefcase, Marple/Tommy.

Clue #4: • at Drew/jewels. **X**s all other detectives for jewels, **X**s for Drew and all other loot. **X** at Drew/Martha and Drew/2nd.

Clue #5: The earliest Brown could be is 3rd, so **X** at Brown/2nd, leaving these possibilities: Brown, 3rd or 4th; Willy, 2nd or 3rd; Nobel, 1st or 2nd. But the gold bar is in the 2nd position! So • for Nobel/1st (**X**s for Nobel at other positions, and other loot at 1st); •s for Willy/2nd and Willy/gold (**X**s for Willy at other positions, Willy/other loot, and gold/other crooks); •s for Brown at 3rd, Brown/Ricky (**X**s for Brown with other crooks, Ricky with other detectives). • Marple/Nobel (**X**s for Marple with other loot, Nobel with other detectives). **X** at Marple/Martha, so • at Marple/Betsy (**X**s for Betsy and other detectives), • at Betsy/Nobel (**X**s for Betsy and other loot, Nobel and other detectives).

So if Brown is 3rd, then Gadget (who can't be 1st, 4th, or 5th) must be 2nd •. Which means the briefcase is 3rd •, and Tommy is 4th. That means Martha has to be 5th • (only blank crook spot in the table), and the secret formula has to be 5th, too •. That leaves Nancy Drew as the only detective left for the 4th slot •, and the jewels are 4th • as well.

1st • Miss Marple • Bad Betsy • Nobel Prize

2nd • Inspector Gadget • Willy the Weasel
  • Solid Gold Bar

3rd • Encyclopedia Brown • Sticky Ricky
  • Briefcase

4th • Nancy Drew • Tommy Trouble • Jewels

5th • Jessica Fletcher • Mad Martha
  • Secret Formula

5. Book of Beginnings
(pages 120–123)

• The Starting Line
50 States in the Union

9 Planets in the Solar System

16 Ounces in a Pound (or in a Pint)

365 Days in a Year

52 Weeks in a Year

10 Years in a Decade

101 Dalmatians

5 Digits in a Zip Code

24 Hours in a Day

7 Colors in the Rainbow

• More Baffling Beginnings
1 Wheel on a Unicycle

4 Quarters in a Football Game

5 Nickels in a Quarter

8 Sides on a Stop Sign

12 Signs of the Zodiac

13 Stripes on the American Flag

18 Holes on a Golf Course

64 Squares on a Chess Board (or a Checker Board)

88 Keys on a Piano

90 Degrees in a Right Angle

1001 Arabian Nights

20,000 Leagues under the Sea

• Completely Confounding Conundrums
1 Small Step for Man, 1 Giant Leap for Mankind

2 Wrongs Don't Make a Right

3 Blind Mice (See How They Run!)

7 Dwarfs in Snow White

10 Frames in a Game of Bowling

1,000 Words that a Picture is Worth

24 Black Birds Baked in a Pie

76 Trombones Led the Big Parade

99 Bottles of Beer on the Wall

200 Dollars for Passing Go in Monopoly

SUGGESTED READING

If you'd like to try more puzzles, check your local library or bookstore for puzzle books. You'll find lots to choose from.

The books listed here are for people who want to do more than just try puzzles. These books tell you how your mind works and where some puzzles came from, how they work, and how you can get better at doing them.

Books for Beginners

Aha! Insight! by Martin Gardner (New York: Scientific American, 1978). An intriguing yet simple exploration of creative problem solving from America's foremost expert on mathematical puzzles.

Alphabet Avenue: Wordplay in the Fast Lane by Dave Morice (Chicago: Chicago Review Press, 1997). A fun guide to the wonderful world of word puzzles.

The Book of Think (or How to Solve a Problem Twice Your Size) by Marilyn Burns (New York: Little, Brown, and Company, 1976). A book about problem solving, written for kids.

Explorabook: A Kids' Science Museum in a Book by John Cassidy and the Exploratorium (Palo Alto, CA: Klutz Press, 1991). This book includes some of our favorite optical illusions, along with lots of great science experiments and all the stuff you need to do them.

Psychology for Kids II by Jonni Kincher (Minneapolis, MN: Free Spirit Publishing, 1995). Forty fun experiments that help you learn about yourself and others. This book includes experiments that deal with memory and visual perception.

The Science Explorer by Pat Murphy, Ellen Klages, Linda Shore, and the Exploratorium (New York: Henry Holt and Company, 1996). This book of experiments for younger kids has more experiments with optical illusions.

Zap Science: A Scientific Playground in a Book by John Cassidy and the Exploratorium (Palo Alto, CA: Klutz Press, 1997). This book includes a section on vision as well as a pair of 3-D glasses.

More-Advanced Reading

These books weren't written for kids, but you might want to give them a try anyway.

Amusements in Mathematics by H.E. Dudeney (New York: Dover Publications, 1970). Originally published in 1917, this book contains more than 400 different mathematical, geometrical, and logical puzzles. Dudeney is considered by some to be the greatest puzzle maker who ever lived.

Creative Puzzles of the World by Pieter Van Delft and Jack Botermans. (Berkeley, CA: Key Curriculum Press, 1995). This book shows you how to make puzzles from paper and wood. A good book for people who like tangrams and toothpick puzzles.

Hexaflexagons and Other Mathematical Diversions: The First Scientific American Book of Puzzles and Games by Martin Gardner (Chicago: University of Chicago Press, 1988). An in-depth look at some fascinating puzzles. Although this book was written for nonmathematicians, Gardner's explanations can be pretty high-level stuff.

New Book of Puzzles by Jerry Slocum (New York: W. H. Freeman, 1992). This book describes mechanical and physical puzzles and how to make them. It includes some puzzle history.

The Oxford A to Z of Word Games by Tony Augarde (Oxford: Oxford University Press, 1996). Anagrams, puns, palindromes, riddles, acrostics—this book is filled with word games of all kinds that draw on examples from the classics of literature.

Visual Games by Franco Agostini (New York: Facts on File Publications, 1986). An interesting exploration of how people communicate with images, including a discussion of optical illusions.

THANK YOU VERY MUCH!

Our thanks to the hundreds of kids and their families who helped the Science-at-Home team explore the Caverns of Memory, the Forest of Hidden Surprises, and the Puzzle House. They tried our experiments and worked our puzzles. We couldn't have finished this book without their help! We would like to thank the following people for exploring with us.

The Abbitt Family
The Adams Family
The Advena Family
The Anand Family
The Anderson Family
The Annis Family
The Asher Family
The Atherholt Family
The Bacca Family
The Baggett Family
The Balk Family
The Barnes Family
The Barry Family
The Barton Family
The Bath Family
The Beckman Family
The Behlen Family
The Benash Family
The Berry Family
Mrs. Kolar's Bigfork Elementary School Grade 4 Sect K
The Blake Family
The Brauning Family
The Brawner Family
The Brennecke Family
The Brenning Family
The Briand Family
The Briggs Family
Ms. Haupt's Britton Area School Class
The Brondyke Family
The Brown Family
The Buenaventura Family
The Bulaevsky Family
The Buoni Family
The Burns Family
The Burns-Griffin Family

The Burrell Family
The Burroughs-Heineman Family
The Carpenter Family
Central Manitoulin, Ontario Public School
The Chang Family
The Chapman Family
The Charles Mack School's 2nd graders
The Chase Family
The Child Family
The Ching Family
The Cifor Family
The Cohen Family
The Coleman Family
The Conknun Family
The Conners Family
The Crabtree Family
The Bruce Dean Family
The Ricky & Cheryl Dean Family
The Delaney Family
The Dorland-Junier Family
The Durham-Williams Family
The Ellerton Family
The Elliser Family
The Engel-Baker Family
The Fairchild Family
The Faneuf Family
The Feldman Family
The Fischman-Quant Family
The Fisher Family
The Flores Family
The Ford Family

The Froke Family
The Frost Family
The Gaar Family
The Gallegos Family
The Gardiner Family
The Gertsch Family
The Giancaspro Family
The Gokhale Family
The Gordon Family
The Gould Family
The Greenberg Family
The Greene Family
The Gubbels Family
The Haddan Family
The Hall Family
The Marie Kay Hamilton Family
The Mary Jane Hamilton Family
The Don Hansen Family
The Karen Hansen Family
The Harpster Family
The Hegland Family
The Hein Family
The Hichner Family
The Hinze Family
The Ho Family
The Horst-Nofziger Family
The Hrubey Family
The Hulse Family
The Huncherick Family
The Hunter Family
The Ijams Family
The Johnson Family
The Johnson-Kuhl Family
The Jones Family

The Judd-Clear Family
The Jue Family
The Kahler Family
The Kelly Family
The Keyser Family
The Kielman Family
The Kim Family
The Klinedinst Family
The Kloess Family
The Kowalczewski Family
The Kremsdorf Family
The Kuch Family
The Kurzweil Family
The Labarile-Koester Family
The Lamb-Chalmers Family
The Landis Family
The Lane Family
The Lanning-Tornquist Family
The Lea Family
The Lee Family
The Lekack Family
The Levy Family
The Logan Family
The Lund Family
The MacCormack Family
The MacLean-Dungy Family
The Maclennan Family
The Maddox Family
The Malenick Family
The Maxwell Family
The McGovern-Cox Family
The McKean Family

The Mell Family
The Menard-Tharp Family
The Messier Family
The Brenda & George Miller Family
The Linda & Michael Miller Family
The Moore Family
The Morgan Family
The Morris Family
The Morsillo Family
The Moss-Stahl Family
The Narigon Family
The Naughton Family
The Neviska Family
The Nilsson Family
The Nunamaker Family
The O'Brien Family
The Offerman Family
The Olacke Family
The Olp Family

The Opotow-Chang Family
The Osborn Family
The Oswalt Family
The Palumbo Family
The Paulson Family
The Pennington Family
The Penston Family
The Perkins Family
The Perry Family
The Peterson Family
The Pianki Family
The Pirtle Family
The Proud Family
The Prudhomme Family
The Pryden Family
The Pukstas Family
The Ramsey Family
The Randall Family
The Reinwald Family
The Riefkohl Family
The Roche Family

The Rockwood Family
The Rosica Family
The Rowen Family
The Ryan Family
The Sandler Family
The Sawicky Family
The Sayles Family
The Schoelen Family
The Schreyer Family
The Schubring-Alcantara Family
The Scornavacca-Wenn Family
Ms. Araque's Sequoia School Class
The Shah Family
The Shoukat Family
The Sobotka Family
The Soucie Family
The Stapleton Family
The Stevenson Family
The Struttmann Family

The Tamm Family
The Thomas Family
The Thorn Family
The Trenchard Family
The Tsang Family
The Tucek Family
The Underhill Family
The Valentine Family
The Vavra Family
The Wallace Family
The Watson Family
The Wildegrube Family
The Wilson Family
The Wolfe Family
The Woodbury Family
The Wright Family
The Yip-SooHoo Family
The Young Family
The Zayas Family

Acknowledgments

The Exploratorium's Science-at-Home team had a lot of help in preparing for and completing our expedition. The experiments, puzzles, games, and activities in this book came from many different sources. Throughout our exploration, people gave us ideas, provided support, tried out our puzzles and experiments, and reviewed what we wrote.

Many people helped us create and test experiments and activities, including Vivian Altmann, Heidi Black, Ruth Brown, Coral Clark, Pablo Dela Cruz, Paul Doherty, Sally Duensing, Ken Finn, Jane Hawkins, Rachel Herz, Thomas Humphrey, Marco Jordan, Karen Kalumuck, Lori Lambertson, Mary Miller, Dean Muller, Eric Muller, Michael Pearce, Don Rathjen, Jonathan Schooler, Jerry Slocum, and Sandy Jackson's science club at the 21st Century Academy. Arthur Shimamura, the principal advisor on the Exploratorium's Memory exhibition, helped us out by reading the manuscript and suggesting corrections. Many Exploratorium staffers helped us recruit families to test our experiments and activities, including Web developers John Fowler and Jim Spadaccini, the hard-working staff of the Exploratorium Store, and the Exploratorium's Explainers.

We'd also like to thank everyone who worked so hard to turn all these ideas into a book. David Sobel at Henry Holt showed us the way into the adventure by suggesting that the book explore places as well as ideas. Larry Antila and David Barker provided graphics support. Megan Bury made sure all our test packets made it to the printer on time, and tabulated the responses from participating families. Judith Brand copyedited the manuscript, ferreting out every inconsistency. Ellyn Hament, our production editor, worked tirelessly to make sure every detail was dealt with and that the process of transforming a manuscript into a book went smoothly. Steve Tolleson, Ellen Elfering, Bill Bowers, René Rosso, and the other creative folks at Tolleson Design helped us figure out how to shape this adventure into book form. Jason Gorski made our imaginary places become real with his amazing pictures.

This book would not have been possible without the moral and administrative support of many people. Thanks to Kurt Feichtmeir for being the keeper of the budget (a thankless but necessary task) and for remaining cheerful through it all. And thanks to Rob Semper and Goéry Delacôte for giving us the institutional backing we needed.

INDEX

-A-
All in the Family story, 101
anagrams, 54–59
  alphabetical order, 57
  antigrams, 57
  changing the consonants, 56
  changing the vowels, 56
  going backwards, 56
  making little words from big words,
    55–56
  making one word or phrase into
    another word or phrase, 57
  making your own, 58
  mixing and matching, 56
  in the newspaper, 59
  party game, 55
angles
  and optical illusions, 79
  and problem solving, 105
antigrams, 57
assumptions
  never make, 99–101, 105, 129
  and shapes, 107
  See also expectations
attitude, and problem solving, 128

-B-
balance, and brain, 131
Barnyard Baffler story, 101
beginnings puzzles, 121–123
bikes logic puzzle, 112–113
blanks. *See* Filling in the Blanks
body position, and brain, 131
brain, parts of the, 130–131
brain stem, 130
brain teasers, 99–101

-C-
cars logic puzzle, 113–114
Case of the 5 Crooks, 116–119
Case of the Baffling Bikes, 112–113
Case of the Messy Room, 111–112
Case of the Mixed-Up Cars, 113–114
Case of the Perplexing Performers, 114–115
cerebellum, 131
cerebral cortex, 131
chess, and Tic-Tac-Toe, 67
chunking, 27–28
colors
  and plexers, 96
  remembering colors of rainbow, 38
comics, and face recognition, 43–44
connecting
  dots, 99
  words, 125–127
context, and pattern recognition, 75
conundrums, completely confounding, 122
coordination, and brain, 131
counting by nine, 39
Crazy Tiles, 80
creativity
  and anagrams, 55
  brain part responsible for, 131
  characteristics of creative people, 125
  and connecting words, 125–127
  and droodles, 33
  and Found Poetry, 126–127
  and Object Masquerade, 127
  and plexers, 97

and problems with multiple answers,
  125–127
and problem solving, 128
and puns, 97
and shape-shifting puzzles, 103
and tangrams, 88
See also imagination
crooks logic puzzle, 116–119

-D-
Dillard, Annie, 127
Dime Tic-Tac-Toe, 65–67
dots, connecting, 99
droodles, 31–33

-E-
eagle tangram, 84–85
emoticons, 44
emotions
  and brain, 131
  and faces, 43–44
expectations, and optical illusions, 81
  See also assumptions
Exploratorium, 144

-F-
face recognition, 43–47
  brain part responsible for, 131
  Emoticons or Smileys, 44
  Faces in the Funnies, 43–44
  Finding Faces Everywhere, 46–47
  Flip-A-Face, 45
Filling in the Blanks, 49–53
  Hangman, 52–53
  Jumping to Conclusions, 49–50
  seeing shapes that aren't there, 51
Fish Flip, 104
flipping
  Fish Flip, 104
  Flip-A-Face, 45
  See also optical flips
fooling your brain. *See* optical flips;
  optical illusions
Found Poetry, 126–127
frontal lobe, 131

-G-
Galileo, and anagrams, 57
geometric shapes. *See* optical flips;
  optical illusions; pattern recognition;
  shape puzzles
Get Your Goat, 105
goat toothpick puzzle, 105
goldfish toothpick puzzle, 104

-H-
Hangman, 52–53
hippocampus, 131

-I-
illusions. *See* optical flips; optical
  illusions
imagination, and memory, 13–15, 24
  See also creativity
impossible answers, and logic puzzles,
  111, 112, 118–119
impossible pictures, 74
impossible stories, 101
It's in the Bag story, 101

-J-
jokes with traps, 100
Jumbles, 59
Jumping Horse story, 101
Jumping to Conclusions, 49

-L-
language equations, 121–123
line optical illusions, 77, 78–79
lion tangram, 86
lists of things, remembering, 23–24
logic puzzles, 111–119
  Case of the 5 Crooks, 116–119
  Case of the Baffling Bikes, 112–113
  Case of the Messy Room, 111–112
  Case of the Mixed-Up Cars, 113–114
  Case of the Perplexing Performers,
    114–115
  tips for solving, 111–112, 113, 114, 118–119

-M-
magic memory tricks, 22
Masquerade, Object, 127
math
  Math Test story, 101
  and Simple Squares, 106–107
  See also numbers
medulla, 130
memory activities, 8–39
  A Is for Apple, B Is for Crab, 21
  brain parts responsible for, 131
  chunking, 27–28
  droodles, 31–33
  and imagination, 13–15, 24
  improving your memory, 12–15, 23–25,
    38–39
  I'm Thinking of . . ., 22
  letters, 28
  lists of things, 23–24
  and long-term memory, 13–15
  for lost memories, 19–25, 38
  and meaning, 29, 31–33
  and mirror images, 20
  multiplying by nine, 39
  names of people, 24–25, 131
  number of days in a month, 39
  numbers, 13, 27–29, 39, 131
  organizing information, 23–24, 25,
    27–28
  party game, 11
  penny recognition, 19–20
  Phantom Words, 36–37
  planets in the solar system, 38
  and pop-up memories, 25
  rainbow colors, 38
  remembering to do something, 38
  remembering where you left
    something, 38
  retrieving memories, 19–25
  rhyming, 38–39
  solitaire, 12, 16
  song recall, 20–21
  spelling tricky words, 38
  telephone numbers, 13, 28–29, 131
  Tell Yourself a Story, 13, 17
  testing your memory, 11–12
  tricking your friends, 22
  tricky memories, 35–39
  Wander Around Your House, 14–15, 17
  and working memory, 13
messy room logic puzzle, 111–112
midbrain, 130
mirror images, and memory, 20
monster optical illusion, 76, 77
months, remembering number of
  days in, 39
moon illusion, 80–81
movement, and brain, 131
multiple answers, problems that have,
  125–127

multiplying by nine, 39
music. *See* songs

-N-
names of people
  anagrams from, 58
  remembering, 24–25, 131
newspapers
  anagrams in, 59
  comics and face recognition, 43–44
numbers
  in jokes with traps, 100
  in language equations, 121–123
  remembering, 13, 27–29, 39, 131
  See also math

-O-
Object Masquerade, 127
One Word Answer, 99
Oppenheimer, Frank, 144
optical flips, 69–75
  and context, 75
  impossible pictures, 74
  seeing double, 69–70
  three-dimensional pictures, 71–73
  why they flip, 73
optical illusions, 76–81
  and expectations, 81
  line illusions, 77, 78–79
  monster illusion, 76, 77
  moon illusion, 80–81
  size illusions, 76–78
  table illusion, 77, 78
  tile illusion, 80
  triangle and square illusions, 51

-P-
pain, and brain, 131
parietal lobe, 131
party games
  anagrams, 55
  memory testing, 11
  Object Masquerade, 127
  tangrams, 87
pattern recognition
  and anagrams, 59
  brain part responsible for, 131
  and context, 75
  face recognition, 43–47
  penny recognition, 19–20
  shape recognition, 51
  and Tic-Tac-Toe, 61, 67
  word recognition, 49–50, 52–53, 59, 75
  See also optical flips; optical illusions
pennies
  recognizing, 19–20
  triangle of, 103–104
perplexing performers logic puzzle,
  114–115
Phantom Words, 36–37
picture illusions. *See* optical flips; optical
  illusions
picture puzzles. *See* shape puzzles
planets, remembering, 38
plexers, 93–97
  examples of, 93, 95
  making your own, 95–97
  and puns, 94, 97
  tips for solving, 94
poetry, found, 126–127. *See also* rhyming
pons, 130
problem solving
  and assumptions, 99, 105, 129
  brain part responsible for, 131
  tips for, 109, 128–129
  See also puzzles
puns, 94, 97

puzzles, 90–127
  anagrams, 54–59
  and assumptions, 99–101
  Brain-Buster Stories, 101
  Case of the 5 Crooks, 116–119
  Case of the Baffling Bikes, 112–113
  Case of the Messy Room, 111–112
  Case of the Mixed-Up Cars, 113–114
  Case of the Perplexing Performers,
    114–115
  connecting words, 125–127
  Fish Flip, 104
  Found Poetry, 126–127
  Get Your Goat, 105
  jokes with traps, 100
  language equations (beginnings
    puzzles), 121–123
  logic puzzles, 111–119
  with multiple answers, 125–127
  Object Masquerade, 127
  One Word Answer, 99
  Penny Triangle, 103–104
  plexers (rebuses), 93–97
  seeing solutions to, 109
  shape puzzles, 82–89, 93–97, 103–109
  Simple Squares, 106–107, 108
  tangrams, 82–89
  tips for solving all puzzles, 109,
    128–129
  tips for solving language-equation
    puzzles, 121–122
  tips for solving logic puzzles, 111–112,
    113, 114, 118–119
  tips for solving shape puzzles, 109
  toothpick, 100, 104–109
  Triangle Challenge, 109
  Tricky Toothpicks, 100
  Tricky Triangles, 108
  why it feels good to solve, 89

-R-
rainbow colors, remembering, 38
rebuses, 93–97
rhyming, and memory, 38–39
riddles, 100
River Rovers story, 101
Road to Confusion, 78

-S-
Science-at-Home Project, 144
seeing double. *See* optical illusions
seeing puzzle solutions, 109
shape puzzles, 103–109
  and assumptions, 107
  Fish Flip, 104
  Get Your Goat, 105
  Penny Triangle, 103–104
  plexers, 93–97
  Simple Squares, 106–107, 108
  tangrams, 82–89
  tips for solving, 109
  Triangle Challenge, 109
  Tricky Triangles, 109
shape recognition. *See* optical flips;
  optical illusions; pattern recognition
Shortz, Will, 123
Simonides's trick, 15
Simple Squares, 106–107, 108
smell sense, and brain, 131
smileys, 44
solitaire, memory, 12, 16
songs, remembering, 20–21
spelling, remembering tricky words, 38
squares
  optical illusion, 51
  Simple Squares, 106–107, 108
  and tangrams, 83–89
Starting Line puzzles, 121–123

stories
  brain-buster, 101
  logic-puzzle, 111–119
  for remembering things, 13, 17
Strange Race story, 101

-T-
table optical illusion, 77, 78
tangrams, 82–89
  eagle tangram, 84–85
  helpful hints for, 85, 86–87, 89
  lion tangram, 86
  making a set of tans, 83
  making your own puzzles, 88–89
  party game, 87
  square tangram, 89
  tangramania, 87
  V is for Victory tangram, 86
  warm-up exercises, 84
telephone numbers, remembering, 13,
  28–29, 131
Tell Yourself a Story, 13, 17
temperature, and brain, 131
temporal lobe, 131
thalamus, 131
Tic-Tac-Toe, 61–67
  benefits of playing, 61, 67
  Dime Tic-Tac-Toe, 65–67
  rules for, 61
  strategies for winning, 62–64, 66–67
  Toe-Tac-Tic, 64
  Wild Tic-Tac-Toe, 64–65
tiles optical illusion, 80
Toe-Tac-Tic, 64–65
toothpick puzzles
  Fish Flip, 104
  Get Your Goat, 105
  Simple Squares, 106–107, 108
  Triangle Challenge, 109
  Tricky Toothpicks, 100
  Tricky Triangles, 108
touch sense, and brain, 131
triangles
  optical illusion, 51
  penny triangle, 103–104
  and tangrams, 83–89
tricky memories
  tricking your friends, 22
  your own, 35–39
tricky perceptions. *See* optical flips;
  optical illusions

-V-
visualizing puzzle solutions, 109
V is for Victory tangram, 86

-W-
Wander Around Your House, 14–15, 17
warped lines optical illusion, 79
Web site, 144
Wheel of Fortune, 53
Wild Tic-Tac-Toe, 64–65
word games
  anagrams, 54–59
  connecting words, 125–127
  context and recognizing words, 75
  Found Poetry, 126–127
  Hangman, 52–53
  Jumping to Conclusions, 49–50
  language equations (beginnings
    puzzles), 121–123
  making numbers into words, 28–29
  One Word Answer, 99
  plexers (rebuses), 93–97
  puns, 94, 97

What is the Exploratorium?

In a residential neighborhood near the Golden Gate Bridge, there's a building filled with flashing lights, machines that buzz and whir, and a constant hum of excited conversation. It's the Exploratorium, San Francisco's world-renowned museum of science, art, and human perception.

Physicist Frank Oppenheimer opened the museum in 1969 as a place where people could find out about science by exploring and asking questions. The mission of his new museum was to let people discover that science is not only understandable, but exciting and fun.

Today, the Exploratorium has more than 600 exhibits—and they all run on curiosity. You don't just look at these exhibits, you play with them. You can touch a tornado, build a bridge, look inside a cow's eye, or leave your shadow on a wall. Every year, more than half a million people from all over the world—including thousands of kids on field trips—come to the Exploratorium to discover for themselves how the world works.

Visit the Exploratorium On-Line at
http://www.exploratorium.edu

The Science-at-Home project hasn't ended with the publication of this book. If you want to find out what we've been up to lately, visit our Web site, where you can learn more about the museum, play with on-line exhibits, learn about our other books, or see what the Science-at-Home team has been up to. To go straight to the Science-at-Home page, type in **http://www.exploratorium.edu/science_explorer.**

Or Come Visit Us in person!

The Exploratorium is located in the Palace of Fine Arts in the Marina District of San Francisco, just south of the Golden Gate Bridge. The next time you're in San Francisco, come by and discover all the amazing activities, exhibits, and special events at the Exploratorium.

What is the Science-at-Home Project?

At the Exploratorium, we think the best way to learn about science is to have fun. But not everyone can come to the Exploratorium to play with our exhibits. So the Exploratorium created the Science-at-Home books that show people how to experiment at home.

The Science-at-Home team has written two books of science experiments for kids: *The Science Explorer* and *The Science Explorer Out and About.* Those books show kids how to experiment with all kinds of stuff—how to make a plane from a drinking straw and paper, how to make amazing structures from gumdrops and toothpicks, how to experiment with shadows and sounds and mirrors.

While we were experimenting, we used all kinds of different things—like tin cans, flashlights, wind-up toys, and sugar cubes. But there was one thing that we used in every experiment. Whether we were taking apart a wind-up toy or making a musical instrument from a stack of tin cans, we were always using our brains. So when it came time to write another book, we decided to explore the amazing gray matter inside our heads.

Like the experiments in the other *Science Explorer* books, each of the experiments in this book was developed at the Exploratorium, then tested by kids from all over the world. Kids told us which experiments worked for them and and which ones didn't. They shared their experiences and made suggestions about how the experiments could be improved.

Through testing, we found out that not everyone likes the same kind of puzzles. Don't be surprised if you really like some puzzles and don't like others. We were the same way—and so were our testers. Some kids loved logic puzzles and didn't care for toothpick puzzles; others loved toothpick puzzles and couldn't understand why anyone would want to do a logic puzzle. So give everything a try, but don't be surprised if you like some things better than others.